"Every couple who values lifelong love must read *Hedges*. In no-nonsense language, Jerry Jenkins provides a clear-cut plan for all of us who want to guard our marriage against sexual saboteurs. This plan is biblical, grounded, realistic, and practical. Don't leave your relationship vulnerable to unnecessary temptation. Plant a protective hedge. Do it today. This book will show you how."

> DR. LES and LESLIE PARROTT, Seattle Pacific University, authors of *Love Talk*

"*Hedges* is a unique book because it doesn't just tell men how to solve their marital problems. Instead it empowers them to build a defensive wall around their marriages, preventing serious problems before they begin."

> JOSH MCDOWELL, author of *More Than a Carpenter*

"When Jerry Jenkins puts words on paper, be certain of this—he has important words to share and he will share them well. That's why we treasure him and his books."

> MAX LUCADO, best-selling author

"Jesus said it Himself, 'There will always be temptation.' Gifted writer Jerry Jenkins gives us all the encouragement to build healthy hedges that protect our marriage and family. Hard-hitting, realistic, and passionate, Jerry provides motivation for married couples to stay intimately close!"

> DR. KEVIN LEMAN, author of *Sheet Music*

"An easy read, practical and captivating. Every couple should read this book. If Christian couples applied the principles of 'hedges,' the divorce rate would be zero. With all my heart, I wish my own father had applied these guidelines. It would have prevented untold misery from the divorce I and my brothers and sisters had to endure from our fractured family, broken because of the lack of hedges."

> ROBERT DANIELS, author of *The War Within: Gaining Victory in the Battle for Sexual Purity*

"*Hedges* is the perfect prescription for our time. With remarkable candor, Jerry Jenkins has penned a blueprint for protecting our marriages. Read it and pass it on to those you care about!"

> DR. GARY and BARBARA ROSBERG, "America's Family Coaches," authors of *Divorce-Proof Your Marriage* and co-hosts of "America's Family Coaches"

HEDGES

JERRY B. JENKINS

HEDGES

LOVING YOUR MARRIAGE
ENOUGH TO PROTECT IT

CROSSWAY BOOKS

A PUBLISHING MINISTRY OF
GOOD NEWS PUBLISHERS
WHEATON, ILLINOIS

Library of Congress Cataloging-in-Publication Data
Jenkins, Jerry B.
    Hedges : loving your marriage enough to protect it /
Jerry B. Jenkins. — Rev. ed.
      p. cm.
    Includes bibliographical references.
    ISBN 1-58134-664-6 (hc : alk. paper)
    1.Marriage—Religious aspects—Christianity. I. Title.
BV835.J46   2005
248.8'44—dc22   2005001131

RRD		14	13	12	11	10	09	08	07	06	05
15	14	13	12	11	10	9	8	7	6	5	4	3	2	1

To DIANNA, of course

Thanks to John Perrodin
for research assistance
and for writing the study guide

CONTENTS

FOREWORD

By Tim LaHaye

Ever since Jerry Jenkins and I met and began our collaboration on the Left Behind series, I have been hearing about hedges. Jerry would frequently talk about the fact that all married couples have a need for hedges. Puzzled at first, I soon realized he wasn't referring to some type of landscaping accessory. No, he was talking about an essential element required to maintain a lifelong marriage relationship. The key was to build hedges around your marriage in order to protect it.

With half of all marriages ending in divorce, there has never been a more critical time than right now for a book such as this. *Hedges: Loving Your Marriage Enough to Protect It* will specifically tell you how to plant hedges against temptations—temptations that can ruin a marriage and bring devastation to a family in the blink of an eye.

The enemies of marriage are all around and are increasing in number every day. Internet porn, chat rooms, and the constant barrage of immoral messages from movies and television are but a few. We are seeing the results of the sexual revolution and moral relativism play out in front of our eyes. Spiritual leaders fall. Our friends, neighbors, and families split up. Pain, suffering, and emotional devastation spiral out of control. Children of divorce not only suffer during childhood but often continue the pattern into their own adult lives.

As I'm sure you know, being a Christian does not eliminate temptation from your life. Quite the contrary. If we look at statistics, Christian marriages are dissolving due to infidelity at a frightening rate. The apostle Paul advises us to flee temptation, which is good advice. Jerry Jenkins takes that admonition from the Bible one step further and gives us practical suggestions on how to plan for and deal with such situations.

Recently my wife, Beverly, and I celebrated our fifty-seventh wedding anniversary. After reading this book, I realized that we had already been practicing many of the recommendations Jerry outlines here. For us, they were something that came from our study of God's Word, and I must say, they have greatly contributed to the continued success and enjoyment of our marriage. But we live in a different culture now. The pressures and temptations coming against marriages today are far worse than when Bev and I first fell in love and promised to stay together for the rest of our lives (or at least until the Lord came!). What was obvious to us fifty-seven years ago has been completely lost on today's generation of married couples.

To some, many of Jerry's suggestions will seem archaic, prudish, and even downright silly. Some may even be tempted to say, "You've got to be kidding!" But that only demonstrates just how far the moral fabric of our society has been torn apart in recent years. Even Jerry himself will admit to feeling somewhat embarrassed when discussing these ideas with others. But the thing is, they work. And with the stakes as high as they are, they are necessary.

Not long ago a friend and his wife, pillars in the Christian community, went through a horrendous divorce. Not only were they and their children emotionally damaged, but the twenty-year-old ministry they had built together was ruined. The wife, who had been praying for reconciliation, appears to have been hit the hardest. And it remains to be seen what lasting impact the divorce will have upon the children. I truly believe that if this couple, particularly the husband, had been practicing the principles outlined in this book throughout their marriage, it never would have ended in divorce.

You may say that your marriage is strong and therefore you have no need for a book such as this. To which I would respond that's all the more reason to read it. You see, this is a book of preventative medicine. Putting into practice its recommendations will insure that your marriage remains strong, healthy, and joyous from here on out.

Thanks, Jerry, for a wonderful book that is at once funny, romantic, eye-opening, biblical, and very helpful.

Tim LaHaye
Author/Minister

INTRODUCTION: MY GIFT

I have a list of rather prudish rules that I used to be embarrassed to speak of except to my wife, to whom they are a gift of love.

These rules are intended to protect my eyes, my heart, my hands, and therefore my marriage. I say these rules appear prudish because my mentioning them when necessary has elicited squints, scowls, and not-so-hidden smiles of condescension. In outlining them here, I risk implying that without following my list, I would plunge into all manner of affairs.

I direct the rules initially toward appearances, because I've found that if I take care of how things look, I take care of how they are. In other words, if I am never alone with an unrelated female because it might not look appropriate, I have eliminated the possibility that anything inappropriate will take place.

In enforcing my own rules I don't mean to insult the many virtuous women who might otherwise have very legitimate reasons to meet or dine with me without the slightest temptation to have designs on me. Simply hedges, that's all these rules are.

As much as people don't like to hear, read, or talk about

it, the fact is that most Christian men do not have victory over lust. I have a theory about that. Scripture does not imply that we ever shall have victory over lust the way we are expected to win over worry or greed or malice. Rather, Paul instructs Timothy, and thus us, not to conquer or stand and fight, or pray about or resolve, but to flee lust.

I know he specifies youthful lust, but I don't believe he's limiting it to a certain age, but rather is describing it, regardless at what age it occurs. The little boy in me will have to flee lust until I flee life.

Think about that. Isn't that freeing? For how many years have we males resolved to quit lusting, to put away impure thoughts, to keep our minds pure regardless of what images the media might offer them? We've turned over new leaves in other areas of our lives. We may have become more sensitive, more helpful, more spiritual, better husbands, better fathers—yes, sometimes in large part because we decided to and applied ourselves.

But this, this dirty little secret, bites when we least expect it and despite all our human efforts. What's wrong with us? Yes, God designed us this way, and yet there are clear biblical mandates against sexual impurity. Trying to conquer lust, and failing, is maddening, frustrating. Until we get the message from Paul that we aren't expected to even try. Don't work at it. Don't study it. Don't pray about it. We're given permission to flee! Head for the hills. Run for your life.

I don't know about you, but that takes a lot of pressure off me. Oh, I'd much rather be known as a mature Christian who is above all that youthful lust. It gives me no pleasure to have to say, sorry, you've got the wrong guy. But at least I don't have to suffer and fail over and over because I just can't manage. I don't have to manage. All I have to do is flee.

That tells me that God understands. He gave me these triggers, these eyes, these hormones, this libido, and not solely for my own gratification. And He designed all this so well that He can't even trust me to be a faithful steward of it. He wants me to be, of course, and He instructs me to be. But in my own strength I fail every time. And instead of condemnation, God offers an out. An escape. Literally. Flee. You've got to love that.

Now, to be realistic, I don't want to be turning tail and running all the time. That's a great out when temptation sneaks up on you, but to me there's wisdom in planning ahead, planting hedges against situations that lend themselves to temptation.

I have planted hedges around myself to protect me, my wife, my family, my employer, my church, and supremely, the reputation of Christ. I share them not to boast, but to admit that I'm still fleeing and in the hope that they might be of some benefit to you.

I'm a layman, a novelist and biographer—not a Bible scholar, psychologist, or counselor. Frankly, that might be an advantage in this endeavor. I'm coming at this as a fellow-struggler, not as an expert. I want to be Bible-based, of course, but not heavily theological and certainly not theoretical. I'll leave the psychology to those so trained and will try to emphasize the practical. Bottom line, I want to provide handles, something to grab on to, something you can use to protect your marriage.

Sad to say, this has never been as crucial as it is today. It wouldn't surprise me if you've lost count—as I have—of the number of friends and relatives and Christian leaders whose marriages have imploded. Surprised that people have fallen to temptation? Hardly. Embarrassed for the church? For the reputation of Christ? Yes. And frustrated that too many have missed the message of Scripture that the escape is easier than they thought: flee.

Let me clarify: My hedges may not be your hedges. You may need to plant some where I never dreamed they would be needed, and vice versa. Resist the urge to get caught up in what a weak, paranoid guy I must be. Rather, if my hedge applies, plant it; if it doesn't, plant one of your own where you need it.

Your marriage, and the church, will be the better for it.

PART ONE

THE NEED FOR HEDGES

*No one thinks he needs them
until it's too late.*

I

THE TANGLED WEB

Sue was not the prettiest and certainly not the sexiest woman John had ever seen. In fact, she didn't hold a candle to his wife. But Sue worked for John. He spent a lot of time with her at the office. He could tell she admired him. He liked her, respected her, and thought she was bright, creative, and interesting. He liked being around her, liked her smile, enjoyed her wit. She was doe-eyed, had perfect teeth, and was married.

Was John romantically interested in her? The question would have offended him. They were both happily married. They didn't even think about an attraction between them. John told his wife about Sue from the day she was hired. His wife was eager to meet Sue and her husband, and the couples genuinely liked each other. The couples didn't socialize frequently because they lived too far from each other, but Sue kept John up-to-date on what was happening in her life, and John told his wife. Sue and John's wife talked on the phone occasionally. John wasn't starry-eyed about Sue, and John's wife had no reason to believe Sue held anything but respect for John.

Which was true.

Was Sue worth losing a home and family over? Now there

was a question even more insulting than the first. No woman was worth that. In fact, John used to tease his wife, "If I ever throw you over, kid, at least I won't humiliate you by running off with a dog."

It was a joke because it was the last thing on his mind. He was a Christian, active in church, a father of three with a comfortable and happy life. He wasn't looking for anything more or different. He was challenged, motivated, and excited about his job and his career path. He was solid. John wasn't even going through a midlife crisis.

So he didn't worry when he first found himself missing Sue when she was out of town for a couple of days. He asked his secretary to be sure to let him know when she called because he had "business to discuss with her." It was true. And when the business had been discussed, they talked a little more.

"We miss you around here, Sue." The emphasis was on "we."

"I miss you too," she said. "All of you. I look forward to seeing you when I get back."

"Me too."

Nice. Friendly. Innocent.

And dangerous. But John didn't know that then.

When Sue returned, her relationship with John changed in subtle ways. During a meeting or in a room full of people they could read each other's eyes in an instant. They weren't reading anything personal. They just knew what the other was thinking about the topic at hand. John could tell when Sue was being circumspect. Sue could tell when John was just being polite, when he didn't really like a proposal but was kind in how he responded to it.

John began to find reasons to be around Sue. He also

found reasons to touch her in a brotherly or even fatherly way—a squeeze of the hand, a touch on the shoulder, a hug of greeting or farewell. He would not have described this as sexual or even sensual. There was no more to it than any man's enjoying physical contact with an attractive, young female.

John was waiting for a cab to the airport as Sue left the office for the day. "The airport's on my way home," she reminded him. "I'll give you a ride."

They talked business on the way. At the curb he looked into her eyes and thanked her warmly. "Any time," she said. He held her gaze for a moment until the humor of her comment sank in. They both smiled. "You know what I mean," she said.

She meant she would do anything helpful for such a good friend. But both also liked the intimate sound of words that could be taken two ways. In the ensuing weeks and months, John and Sue began slowly to depend upon each other emotionally. He told her things no one else in the office knew: his dreams, his plans, his private ambitions, his assessments of others. They went from telling each other what good friends they were to making their conversation more personal, more meaningful. He called her his "favorite friend." She often told him he was "special."

Theirs wasn't a dual pity party, bad-mouthing their spouses or looking to the other for ingredients missing in their marriages. No, they were simply two people who hit it off, liked each other, became special to each other, and eventually became enamored with each other. Suddenly, or so it seemed, the inevitable happened.

They justified a few lunches and even a working dinner.

When their bodies touched while in a cab or in a restaurant booth, neither pulled away. It was natural, familiar. Brotherly and sisterly. When he touched her arm while talking to her, he often left his hand there even after his point had been made.

At a convention out of town, even with six others from their office along, they found opportunities to be alone together. It wasn't easy, and though their relationship had not escalated to the declaring stage yet, they both knew. There was no one either would rather be with. After a late dinner with everyone from their office, she called his room and said she couldn't sleep.

"I'm not tired either," he said, lying. He had collapsed into bed after the long day. "What do you want to do?"

"I don't know. Just talk."

"So talk."

"You wanna go for a walk?"

They met in the lobby and strolled the deserted city streets. She thought her sweater would be enough, but the summer night grew chilly after midnight, and as they crossed a bridge over the river, he slipped his suit jacket over her shoulders. She smiled at him in the moonlight, and he put his arm around her. She slipped her hand around his waist. They walked silently for twenty minutes until they came to a dark spot between street lights.

John slowed to a stop, his emotions racing. Sue looked quizzically at him, but when he took her in his arms, they embraced so naturally, so perfectly that it seemed right. He could feel her heart pounding. "Dare I kiss you?" he whispered in her hair.

She held him tighter, as if stalling to decide. "Your call," she said, mimicking his favorite expression to subordinates. It was all he needed to hear.

Theirs was one long, soft, meaningful kiss that spoke volumes. They stared into each other's eyes for a slow moment, then headed back to the hotel, his hand gently on her arm. As the building came into sight, Sue stopped. "We have to talk."

"I know."

"What are you thinking, John?"

"The same thing you're thinking."

"Don't be too sure."

"I'm sure, Sue."

"You first, boss."

"This will never work, Sue. It didn't happen. We go back to our respective rooms good friends who happen to like each other very much."

Her eyes filled. "You know me too well."

"I'm relieved, Sue. I certainly didn't intend this, and I don't want to mislead you."

"The walk was my idea, but I didn't have this in mind."

"Nothing happened, Sue. Deal?" He stuck out his hand.

She shook it but held on. "Why do I want to kiss you again, John? I agree we have to end this, but it seems so incomplete."

"I feel the same way. But we cannot. We must not."

"I know," she said, dropping his hand. She smiled bravely and headed into the elevator.

John stared at the ceiling until 4 in the morning, dredging up every negative detail of his marriage. In twelve years he and his wife had become known as a successful and happy couple. By the time he gave up trying to sleep, however, he had convinced himself that he had never loved her, that the marriage was a mistake, and that he felt something for Sue he had never felt for any other woman, including—and especially—his wife.

Jaw set and mind whirling, John strode to the window and gazed into the darkness. Was that Sue sitting on the low concrete wall in the courtyard below?

John freshened up and dressed quickly. He took the stairs to the ground floor and exited a side door. Sue started when she first saw him. Then she sat still and stared ahead, as if resigned that this meeting was somehow inevitable.

"Sue, are you all right?"

She nodded and dabbed at her face. "I just have to get over this."

"Anything I can do?"

She shook her head. "It's not going to be easy working with you."

"It doesn't have to be difficult, Sue. We just need to back up a few months. We're friends, and we can enjoy that, can't we?"

"You make that sound easy, John. I can't."

"Why not?"

She took a deep, quavery breath and fought for composure. She still hadn't looked at him. "I'm in love with you, John. That's why."

He reached for her, and she came to him. They embraced and kissed, and he told her he loved her too. He led her back into the hotel the way he'd come, avoiding the lobby and the elevators. They trudged up the stairs to her room. He left there two hours later, in time to prepare for the day.

John and Sue shared a delicious, bleary-eyed secret for

the rest of the convention. They spent most of every night together, and there was no more talk of how things would have to change when they traveled back home to reality.

John and Sue convinced themselves that their love was so perfect that God had to be in it. Neither was prepared for the vehement reactions from their spouses and extended families. The anger, the confusion, the accusations drove them closer to each other. Within six months both divorces were final, and John and Sue were married. A year later, while Sue was pregnant with her first child, John announced he had made a terrible mistake. He wanted his wife and family back, and he set upon such an impractical and obnoxious approach that he lost his job and his new wife. In the process he permanently alienated himself from his former wife as well.

SURELY NOT THEM!

John and Sue's story is representative of several I've heard from friends, relatives, and acquaintances. It has become so common that I cringe when someone says, "Did you hear about so-and-so?" They may be informing me of a move or an award or a new job or a new baby, but my first dreaded thought is, *Oh no, please, not them too.* All too often my worst fears are confirmed. No one is immune. The strongest marriage you know of is in danger today if hedges are not in place.

I recently reminisced with several old friends. Every one of us knew personally of several painful marriage failures due to infidelity. Even more appalling, nearly all of us could point to incidents among our close relatives. Can anyone still doubt there is an epidemic of divorce, even within the church and, sadly, rampant even among so-called Christian leaders?

In a strange way, the problem is exacerbated in the Christian community because unfaithful spouses are generally not in danger—the way the secular community is—of contracting AIDS or herpes. The type of person I'm writing about is not characteristically promiscuous. John, in the above example, had never before slept with a woman other than his wife. Ironically, while the secular world is cleaning up its act due to fear of deadly disease, Christians blithely proceed, unaware they need hedges to protect them from surprise attacks in their areas of sexual weakness.

Try an informal survey on your own. Ask friends and relatives how many people they know who have fallen to sexual temptation. Perhaps you don't need to ask. Maybe you know firsthand more such stories than you care to recount. If those people were vulnerable, who else might be? Who will be next about whom you say, "I never would have dreamed he would do such a thing"? You know these people. You have to wonder what made them fall. What made them vulnerable?

LITTLE FOXES

Just as it's the little foxes that spoil the vine, so seemingly small indiscretions add up to major traps. John and Sue allowed themselves to admire, like, respect, and enjoy each other without giving a second thought to the progression of feelings, the danger of developing emotional feelings, or the lure of infatuation. They never reminded themselves of their wedding vows, because they had no intention of breaking them. Feelings and emotions sneaked up on them when they least expected it, and then it was too late.

Look at the account of David's failure in 2 Samuel 11. Here was a man after God's own heart. Have you ever wondered why he didn't go to battle? Scripture doesn't provide a lot of detail about this incident, but the question arises: Was David too old, too tired, too successful, or too something to lead his army? Or was there some subconscious, or not so subconscious, maneuvering to get himself into a position where he could get next to Uriah's wife?

Why did he take a walk on his veranda that day? Was Bathsheba not aware that her bath was within sight of the king's palace? An innocent walk and a bath in the open air could be considered nearly innocent indiscretions. Give Bathsheba the benefit of the doubt, but David should have turned away when he saw a naked woman. The fact that even a man after God's own heart was unable to do that lends credence to the theory that we are to flee rather than to try to conquer lust.

Inviting the wife of your commanding officer over after seeing her bathe must be considered more than a small indiscretion. Despite my respect for a man of God, I have to suspect David's motives. Could he simply have wanted to get better acquainted? There's an understatement. He knew this woman. She was married to one of his high-ranking soldiers and lived in the neighborhood. Did David know when he invited her that he would sleep with her that night? Surely he wasn't testing his resolve to remain pure before God. What Bathsheba knew or didn't know we can scarcely guess. In that time, a summons from the king was disobeyed only under the threat of death. So from the time she received his invitation, her fate was sealed.

Safe to say, had it not been for the initial indiscretions, adultery may never have resulted. And look at what happened after that. Bathsheba became pregnant. David called

Uriah home from battle in the hope that he would sleep with his wife and believe the child was his own. Uriah, a man of honor (how must that have made David feel?), refused to enjoy the comforts of his home and his wife while his men were in battle. Had Uriah slept with his wife, David would have fostered deceit. As it turned out, Uriah's sense of duty drove David to have him killed. Scripture tells how David sent the Hittite back to war with his own death notice in his hand (2 Samuel 11:14-17).

CLOSE ENCOUNTERS OF THE WORST KIND

How close have you come to being burned? Have you found yourself impressed with someone and then attracted to her? Maybe it seemed innocent and safe, but then you said or did things you never thought you would say or do. Maybe on a business trip you hung around with a colleague of the opposite sex, and upon reflection you know you wouldn't have wanted your spouse to do the same thing. It could be that nothing improper was said or done, but simply investing the emotional energy and time was inappropriate. Maybe, looking back, you see you were living dangerously. When friends fall right and left, you recognize you were lucky that you weren't ensnared.

Or maybe you did become emotionally or even physically involved and fell just short of committing adultery. Perhaps you live with guilt because you never confided that to anyone, including—and especially—your spouse.

If so many of your friends and acquaintances have fallen—people you never would have suspected—how will you avoid being a casualty?

2

THE CHANGING CLIMATE

There's a new openness to interaction between the sexes in the workplace, in the neighborhood, in counseling—even in the church. Christians touch more, speak more intimately, are closer to one another. There are advantages to this but also grave dangers. Fear can be good.

Dr. Tim LaHaye and I have been asked if we think it's fair, in our Left Behind novels, to use fear to scare people into the kingdom. Frankly, I think some things need to be feared. An eternity without God is one. Dianna and I raised three sons, and I wasn't above scaring them about things they should be afraid of. I told them that if they played in the street, they risked being run over. That if they played near the charcoal grill, they risked horrible burns. That if they played with the electrical outlet, they risked electrocution.

And fear is as good a motivator as any to maintain fidelity.

In a survey conducted by Christianity Today International (CTI) researchers, of one thousand male readers (non-pastors) of *Christianity Today*, fully 23 percent indicated they had engaged in sexual intercourse with someone other than their wives. Twenty-eight percent indicated they had involved themselves in other forms of sexual contact outside their marriages. In a separate survey of pastors, 23 percent said they had done something sexually inappropriate outside their marriages, 12 percent indicating adulterous intercourse.[1]

Ready for this? The above research was conducted more than fifteen years ago! Internet porn was in its infancy then. In 2001 the CTI magazine *Leadership's* "Survey on Pastors and Internet Pornography" found that four in ten pastors online have visited a pornographic web site, more than one-third of those within the previous twelve months. *Leadership* also reported this response to the statistics: From non-pastors: "So many!" From pastors: "Is that all?"[2]

Frankly I hesitate to share such findings. On the one hand they shed light on an epidemic. On the other, is there not a risk of providing justification? Might not a man be tempted to rationalize, "Even my pastor slips, so it's no big deal if I do too"?

Knowing we're not alone in this struggle can make it easier to consent to accountability. Men who admit their weaknesses to one another gain strength and amass weapons against temptation. They find themselves able to talk openly about what people like the couple in the first chapter could have done to insure against the misery they brought upon themselves.

I make myself accountable to close male friends, and we pledge to punch the other in the mouth if we ever run roughshod over our sacred vows. But beyond that, we ask each other the tough questions: Are you staying true to your wife? Are you avoiding dangerous situations? Are you able to flee temptation?

Close friends and even relatives and loved ones report real victory through the hedge of accountability.

Probably the greatest change in society since I first began planting hedges more than fifteen years ago is the easy, private accessibility of pornography via the Internet. Again, while we'd all like to believe we are above such a base temptation, the statistics above reveal otherwise. (Not to mention, we know ourselves.) Fleeing this lure, if it happens to be one that troubles you, begins well in advance. Don't go to a web site that can titillate you with sample images, rationalizing that at least you didn't pay to see anything worse. Anyone who has even happened upon these sites accidentally knows that the advertising alone far exceeds the bounds of propriety for a Christian.

It's amazing how many Christians have been ensnared, caught, and even fired for accessing Internet porn on the job. Imagine the humiliation and pain to the families, let alone to the individual himself.

There's nothing complicated about the hedge that needs to be planted here. Go to a web site such as this one: http://www.filterreview.com/ and follow the simple instructions for slamming the door on this poison. You should find that the earlier such decisions are made for you, the more successful you'll be in fleeing.

Other helpful resources include Covenant Eyes, a web-based program that monitors how you use your computer and will e-mail a notice to your accountability partners should you log onto a porn site. Check this out for yourself at www.covenanteyes.net/about-how.php.

Another web site worth investigating and highly recommended is http://www.internetfilterreview.com/resources.html.

Focus on the Family offers Internet filter recommendations at www.family.org. At their site, simply type "internet filters" in the search window.

BACK TO JOHN AND SUE

The types of second marriages that evolve out of situations like John and Sue's seldom work; but make no mistake, had their marriage been idyllic, the entire situation still would have been disastrous for their previous spouses, John's children, and both extended families.

First, both should have been aware of the potential danger and recognized the infatuation for what it was. This is basic, though not admitted by most Christians. It simply is not uncommon in the workplace to meet someone with whom there seems an immediate bonding. You like her, she likes you, you hit it off. That is the time to deal with the problem, because it can become a serious dilemma.

You can be married ten years and still develop a crush on someone. You think about her, find yourself talking about her, quoting her (even to your spouse), and generally become enamored with her. The 1988 Christianity Today International (CTI) survey showed clearly that the major factor contributing to extramarital relationships is physical and emotional attraction (78 percent), far outdistancing marital dissatisfaction (41 percent).[3]

That is the time to remind yourself that this is nothing more than an adult version of adolescent puppy love, and it will pass. It really will. The person is off-limits, and you should run from the situation as from a contagious disease.

You may still see the person in the work setting, and you may still enjoy proper interaction with her. But ground rules need to be set. Never tell the person that you are attracted to her. Talk about your spouse frequently in front of her. Tell your spouse about the person, but use your own judgment as to how fully to explain your dilemma. I have a friend who seems to delight in telling his wife about all the women upon whom he develops such instant and fleeting crushes. He encourages her to do the same, but while she admits she is susceptible to similar experiences, she prefers not to talk about them or to hear about his. My own wife is fully aware of my hedges, and thus she is not threatened by my extolling the appropriate virtues of a colleague. Of course, I don't rhapsodize about someone's looks or say stupid things like, "If I had met her before I met you . . ."

When you first become aware of the impact the other person has on you, that is the time to move into action. You should be able to determine the extent of the danger a person represents to you by your own body language, how you sit or stand when talking with her, how much eye contact seems acceptable, whether you seem magnetized by her, and how much you look forward to seeing her.

Don't treat your new friend the way you would an old, respected friend. Refrain from touching her, being alone with her, flirting with her (even in jest), or saying anything to her you wouldn't say if your spouse were there. (While you may not be so rigid in your conduct with a long-time friend of the opposite sex, beware. Certain guidelines must still be enforced. Friendships, especially with long-admired associates, can turn intimate even more quickly than new alliances.)

So, what could John and Sue have done? Had either realized they were becoming enamored with each other, they could have shifted gears, gone into a protective mode, and saved themselves from ruining many lives.

If hedges are planted early enough, preferably well in advance of even meeting someone else, they can be painless and can nip marriage-threatening relationships before they get started. That's why we so desperately need practical suggestions on how to plant impenetrable boundaries around our marriages.

If you can believe *The Hite Report on Male Sexuality*,[4] which I don't recommend reading or believing, nearly three-fourths of married men cheat on their wives. Admittedly, the responses were from people with enough interest in the subject to answer a multi-page questionnaire that gave them the opportunity to discuss sex in the most pedestrian and vulgar terms, generally robbing it of any sacred mystery. In fact, the monumental report itself (1,129 pages in hardback) could be enlisted as a masturbatory aid, if one was so inclined. A huge percentage of the respondents were apparently so inclined, as evidenced in their comments.

On the subject of adultery, the author summarizes:

> The great majority of married men were not monogamous. Seventy-two percent of men married two years or more had had sex outside of marriage; the overwhelming majority did not tell their wives, at least at the time [of the incidents].[5]

Given the unscientific, nonrepresentative nature of the research, the above quotation can be taken with a healthy dose of sodium, but it should be pointed out that a significant number of respondents referred to themselves as born-again Christians. Putting this body of research with the CTI survey provides a rough idea where the Christian community fits in the overall scheme of marital faithfulness.

The Barna Update of November 3, 2003, "Morality Continues to Decay," reports that a study of what Americans believe is moral and immoral reveals that nearly half the population thinks sex outside marriage is okay.[6]

When a famous television evangelist announced he was stepping aside from his ministry because of an affair, I shook my head. I had never been a follower of the man, but I had been bemused by his apparently confused set of values. Sadly, the news of his moral failure was thus not a surprise. Further revelations included gross financial mismanagement, empire building, and even homosexuality.

Another Christian television personality's moral failure included a lifelong fascination with pornography and an apparent attempt to get as close as possible to extramarital sex without actually committing it. *Christian Parenting Today* (also a CTI publication), in a Summer 2003 article entitled "Poison Control" by Michelle Lippincott, reports that Russell Willingham, a pastoral counselor and the author of *Breaking Free: Understanding Sexual Addiction & the Healing Power of Jesus* (InterVarsity Press), found that between 40 and 65 percent of Christian men struggle with pornography.[7]

Hearing of the ruined ministries of television evangelists due to sexual immorality is one thing. Seeing the same happen to your neighbor, your friend, or a family member is something else altogether. It may be hard to identify with the man who has everything—a ministry, wealth, status, popularity, a beautiful family—and risks it all for a season of pleasure, but it is not hard to identify with the man next door. Or in the mirror.

When your assistant pastor, brother-in-law, or best friend from college falls, that's too close to home. Then you get to see at close range the tumble of dominoes set in motion by infidelity.

THE PRICE

Infidelity. What a genteel word for what it describes. Such a word goes down easier than violating one's trust, breaking one's marriage vows, being unfaithful, sleeping around, fornicating, committing adultery. But using a mild word for sin doesn't change a thing.

I was twelve years old when I was first affected by the ravages of immorality. Something was wrong in the only church I had ever known, and no one would tell me what was going on. There were meetings, public and private, charges, accusations, arguments, tears, factions. I badgered and bugged and bothered until I forced my mother to tell me what I later wished I didn't know.

"You're too young to deal with it."

"No, I'm not, Mom. I'm twelve!" How old that sounded at the time!

"You'll wish you hadn't asked."

"Just tell me! Please!"

"You wouldn't believe it."

"Yes, I will! Tell me!"

"Would you believe me if I told you that our pastor doesn't love his wife anymore?"

"No!"

"See?"

It couldn't be true. The pastor and his wife were perfect! They had four biological children and had adopted another. I had looked up to and admired and respected them for as long as I could remember.

A young married woman in the church had been the center of the rumors. Was there an affair? Had someone seen them embrace? Could the stories be true of the pastor berating his wife? My head swam as the rumors flew.

The pastor's final sermon was a not-so-veiled admission of a mistake, but not adultery. He was confessing an error from years before—his choice of a wife. Even those who refused to believe the charges of adultery expressed horror over that public humiliation of his mate.

The church was ravaged by a near-split soon after his departure. Then came the news of the divorce. That little church was left in pieces, and it took years to pull itself back together.

I was young and naive enough to believe no such trauma had ever before hit a wonderful church like ours, nor could it ever happen again. Since then I have heard countless such stories about pastors and have lived through more—including both a senior pastor and an assistant pastor I had sat under. One left notes for his trusted friends and associates, praising God for "this new, divine love that is so wonderful that the Lord had to author it." Another friend tried to convince me that the relationship that broke up both his and his mistress's marriages was "in the center of God's will."

THE ROOT

What seemed an aberration more than forty years ago in a small town was merely a harbinger for the marital devastation that has hit the Christian community today. Pollster George Barna and Mark Hatch, in their book *Boiling Point: How*

Coming Cultural Shifts Will Change Your Life, report that one of four adults "who have ever been married has also experienced a divorce—and, amazingly, the incidence of divorce is slightly higher among born-again Christians than among others [27 percent vs. 24 percent]."[8]

Marriages are breaking up at such an alarming rate that it's hard to find someone who has not been affected by divorce in his immediate family. How many can you count in your own family, including grandparents on both sides, aunts, uncles, and your own siblings?

You may not know how many of those divorces were the result of immorality, but half is a fair assumption. Women leave their husbands for a variety of complex reasons, the most minor of which—according to marriage counselors—is their own lust. Rarely do you hear of a woman who simply fell for someone who, by his sexual appeal alone, turned her head and heart from her own husband.

But men—yes, even those who would blame their frumpy, crabby, boring wives for their own roving eyes—don't really need an excuse. They point to myriad reasons for having to leave, but it nearly always can be traced to lust, pride, and a false sense of their own strength. Remember that the major factors leading to the illicit relationships in the 1988 CTI survey showed 78 percent of respondents citing physical and emotional attraction, while only 41 percent cited marital dissatisfaction.[9]

Think of the men you know and the reasons they gave for finding someone new. Did some have incredibly attractive, even sexy wives? Can all those men complain of their wives' frigidity? And even if they could, does this in any way excuse the breaking of their sacred vows?

My own experience in trying to counsel straying husbands reveals a strange bent. A man who has cheated on his wife often invents reasons after the fact. The man who once taught marriage seminars, raved about his wife, treated her right, and was proud of her now must say:

- "We hid the truth. Our marriage was never good."
- "In private she was not what she appeared to be in public."
- "I never really loved her."
- "She didn't understand me" (the oldest saw in the tool kit).
- And one more that became my favorite excuse to hate: "Actually, I disobeyed God by marrying her in the first place."

NO EXCUSE

We've all heard the adage that every broken marriage has two sides and that there's no such thing as a completely innocent party. However, those statements need examination. True, none of us knows what went on behind closed doors, and we all know how base we can be in private, compared to the image we like to project.

But if you know divorced couples, you know of examples where, even if the wife was not entirely innocent, she was certainly not guilty of anything that justified her husband's leaving her. I've been acquainted with enough such offending men to see their defenses coming a mile away. Suddenly this woman we all know as a wonderful person— not perfect, maybe a bit dull, maybe harried and overworked, maybe not as dazzling as she was when they first married—is now painted as a monster. This from the man who is no prize himself, and yet he has justified breaking the laws of God, breaking his promises to his wife, violating their union, and blaming it on her!

I once knew a denominational leader in his sixties who carried on a year-long affair with a younger woman. When he was exposed and defrocked and called before his superiors, he brought along his wife, who took full responsibility. No confession from him. No apology. It was her fault, he said. She said it herself.

Call it what you will, but a man with as perfect a wife as he could ever want is still capable of lust, of a senseless seeking of that which would destroy him and his family. If he does not fear his own potential and plant a hedge around himself and his marriage, he's headed for disaster.

A HEALTHY FEAR

Shall we all run scared?

Yes! Fear is essential.

"There are several good protections against temptation," Mark Twain said, "but the surest is cowardice."[10]

Look around. Let your guard down, don't remind yourself that you made a vow before God and men, don't set up barriers for your eyes, your mind, your hands, your emotions, and see how quickly you become a statistic.

A man may say, "It could never happen to me. I love my wife. We know each other inside and out by now. We've left the emotional infatuation stage that ruled our courtship and honeymoon, and we love God's way: unconditionally and by the act of our wills. We each know the other is not perfect, and we accept and love each other anyway. We're invulnerable to attack, especially by lust that leads to immorality."

But when that man falls—because he has not planted

hedges to protect himself—his tune changes. His excuse becomes that he fell out of love, the old magic was gone, the wife got too busy with the house and kids, his needs were not being fulfilled.

Worse, the Christian deserter becomes so infatuated with his new love that he often gives God the credit. Know a counseling pastor or a Christian psychologist? Ask him how many times he's heard a man say, "This new relationship is so beautiful, God has to be behind it." Never mind that it goes against all sense and every tenet of Scripture, not to mention everything the man has ever believed in and stood for.

A friend hit me with that excuse once, and I quickly moved farther from him to another chair. He looked at me in surprise. "If God strikes you with lightning for that," I said, "I'd rather not be so close."

What is happening? Okay, I'm an aging baby boomer. When I was in elementary school I knew one, maybe two kids from broken homes. Divorce among church people was almost nonexistent. Now the solid, happy marriage is the exception. From people we never dreamed would have problems come stories of affairs, adultery, separation, and divorce.

Ever notice how many middle-aged people in your church seem to have unusually young families? The divorce stigma still exists. So do you suppose many divorced and remarried people just move on to a new church and never mention that previous families—from both sides—were left behind? I'm not implying that people in this situation should not be welcomed and allowed to worship and rebuild their lives. Just that there are likely many more such couples than we know.

This is not the forum in which to debate the issue of

divorce. Scripture is clear that God hates divorce (Malachi 2:16), but opinions vary as to whether He forbids it altogether or allows it in only one or two circumstances, and whether remarriage is allowed regardless of the reason for the divorce.

No matter where you stand on those issues, you must agree that no one marries intending or wanting to divorce. Some, no doubt, from the beginning consider divorce a convenient option and vow to stay together for as long "as we both shall love." But even the Christian with the most liberal position possible on divorce says and means at his wedding that he is pledging himself to his wife forever. He may later forget it or decide that it was merely archaic formality, but there's no way around it. His vows were legal, sacred, and moral. When he commits adultery, he breaks his promise.

One of the most effective ways to deal with a friend trying to justify his adultery is to say, "Bill, don't forget that I was there. I heard you say it. I heard you promise that you would take no one but Jane unto yourself for as long as you both shall live."

"Yeah, but—"

"You can 'yeah, but' all you want, but the fact is, you broke your promise."

"But she—"

"Regardless what she did or didn't do, you broke your promise, didn't you?"

That can take the wind out of any sail made out of excuses.

RUN, DON'T WALK

A complex litany of events takes place between the vows and the adultery, and it behooves those of us who want to remain pure to examine those events, expose them for what they are, and either avoid letting them happen or avoid letting Satan use them to lure us into justifying our sin.

Once we have identified them, what will we do about them? Will we pray over them? Resolve to conquer them? Turn over new leaves? Ironically, the answer is easier than that. As I've said, according to one liberating bit of Scripture, we are not to win, not to gain the victory, not to succeed by the sheer force of our wills, our consciences, or our determination.

> Flee also youthful lusts: but follow righteousness, faith, charity, peace, with them that call on the Lord out of a pure heart. (2 Timothy 2:22, KJV)

We are to run. To flee. To get out. To get away. Why? Does this admonition to flee somehow serve as an admission on God's part that He did not even equip us with the ability to subdue our natures in this area? The question is valid. Concerning adultery, in the Old Testament God tells us, "You shall not . . ." (Exodus 20:14), and in the New Testament He says that if we so much as look upon a woman to lust after her, we have already committed adultery with her in our hearts (Matthew 5:28).

In other areas, God grants us victory. We can win over jealousy, a bad temper, greed, and even pride. We can train our consciences to avoid theft, bad-mouthing, and lying. But do you know anyone who could avoid a peek at pornography if convinced no one would find out?

ProtectKids.com reports more than 1.3 million porn web sites with more than 260 million web pages and growing (a twenty-fold increase between 1998 and 2003 alone). In

September 2003 alone, more than thirty-two million individuals visited a porn site, 71 percent of them male.[11]

Clearly there are times when we are stronger than at other times. So what are we to do when temptation rages? If we are weak and have not taken precautions, if we have not applied preventive medicine, we have already failed. The only answer is to plan, to anticipate danger, to plot the escape.

The time to plant hedges is before the enemy attacks.

NOTES

1. "How Common Is Pastoral Indiscretion?" *Leadership* (Winter 1988), 12-13.
2. "The Leadership Survey on Pastors and Internet Pornography," *Leadership* (Winter 2001).
3. "How Common Is Pastoral Indiscretion?" 13.
4. See Shere Hite, *The Hite Report on Male Sexuality* (New York: Alfred Knopf, 1981).
5. Ibid.
6. "Morality Continues to Decay," *The Barna Update*. November 3, 2003. http://www.barna.org/FlexPage.aspx?Page=BarnaUpdate& BarnaUpdateID=152.html
7. "Poison Control," *Christian Parenting Today*. Summer 2003. Citing Russell Willingham, *Breaking Free: Understanding Sexual Addiction & the Healing Power of Jesus* (Downers Grove, IL: InterVarsity Press, 1999).
8. George Barna and Mark Hatch, *Boiling Point: How Coming Cultural Shifts Will Change Your Life* (Ventura, CA: Regal Books, 2001), 49.
9. "How Common is Pastoral Indiscretion?" 13.
10. Mark Twain, *Following the Equator*, Vol. 1, "Pudd'nhead Wilson's New Calendar," Chapter 36.
11. Donna Rice Hughes, ProtectKids.com, November 1, 2004. http://www.protectkids.com/index.html

3

DON'T BLAME GOD

One of the most fascinating and misunderstood differences between men and women is in their thought processes and sexual triggers. I was in the eighth grade when short skirts became popular. I thought I'd died and gone to heaven. Our school went through ninth grade, so to me, ninth-grade girls were women. Of course, in 1962-63, what I considered short skirts were just an inch or two above the knee. Lord, have mercy! The trend would escalate to micro-minis by the time I reached college; so I spent my entire adolescence with my eyes open.

I suppose that era made me a leg man, though it would be a lie to say that any other female physical attribute is far down my appreciation list. Lest I sound like a wolf-whistling lecher, please know that this was a private sport. While we junior high boys might nudge someone so he could follow our eyes to a choice target, for some reason we didn't admit to each other how deeply we felt about looking at girls.

Indeed, I thought I was probably the only Christian boy attracted to the female figure. From childhood on I had read in a denominational magazine letters from teenagers lamenting having gone too far in their relationships and pleading for advice on how to control themselves. That turned out to be a good foundation for me when I began dating and facing temptation. I credit that early input—along with dating virtuous women—for coming to my wedding night as virginal as my bride: wholly.

Yet in junior high and high school I feared I would wind up as one of those letter writers. I was so enamored with women and their sensual beauty that I was convinced I had the potential to become a fiend. When I realized that even more exciting to me than any sports drama was watching a girl cross her legs and catching a glimpse of thigh, I knew I had it bad.

Had I only known this was normal! That I was not alone! That such attraction to women, yes, even to their sexuality, was God's idea! Is that heresy? It's not now, and it wasn't then. Though I can't recall having completely lustful thoughts in junior high, I carried a deep sense of guilt about even wanting to look at girls. As best I can recall, I had no thoughts of illicit sex. Still, I felt guilty. Something seemed wrong with thinking about this all the time. What a relief it would have been to discover that (depending on which expert you read) the typical American adolescent male thinks about sex no fewer than four times every minute!

Of course, as I graduated from puberty and went on for a master's degree in girl watching, it became more and more difficult to separate looking and appreciating from lusting. It was only small comfort to me when I heard a Christian youth leader say that 99 percent of all heterosexual boys have a problem with lust and that the other 1 percent are liars. I was devout in my faith and knew right from wrong; yet I seemed to have no control, no resolve, no victory in this area. I regret not having had an adult perspective that would have allowed me to enjoy those years with wonder and without guilt.

With my own three sons, I allowed for the natural attraction to and preoccupation with females, and we talked about it rather than pretending there was something wrong with it. I sometimes cautioned them about thoughts, and we discussed openly the priceless value of their goal to reach marriage without having fallen into sexual sin.

Beyond that I didn't pretend that they should chastise themselves for appreciating a form designed by God to attract them. Without being crude, we discussed which girl in an ad or on a television program was most attractive and why. I admitted that women were still fun to look at, even at my ripe age. They probably got tired of my cautioning them to be careful about dwelling on the sexual and to simply admire, delight in, enjoy, and respect God's beautiful creativity.

Drs. Miriam and Otto Ehrenberg classify parents in four categories according to their views of sex in raising their children: Sex Repressive (sex is bad and should be discussed or dealt with only in that light), Sex Avoidant (sex is OK but is best not talked about), Sex Obsessive (sex is everything; no taboos; even young children should be conversant about it), Sex Expressive (sex is good and healthy and should be discussed appropriately).

They write:

> The aim of Sex Repressive parents is very specific: to curb sexual behavior and keep their children, especially their daughters, away from sexual entanglements before they are married. The impact of Sex Repressive parents, however, goes way beyond this goal. They instill a sense of shame in children about their innate sexuality which alienates children from their parents and interferes with their later capacity to form satisfying rela-

tionships with the opposite sex. . . . Children in these circumstances grow up feeling bad about the sexual stirrings which
are an essential part of their nature, and resentful towards their
parents for disapproving of this very basic aspect of their
being.[1]

Any conscientious parent would want to be Sex Expressive,
but for Christians, there is a major problem with this secular
view of sexuality. While it is almost always positive and healthy
to be Sex Expressive, we must also instill in our children the
biblical admonition that sex before or outside of marriage is
wrong, is sin, and has consequences. In other words, during the
time of our children's peak sexual awareness—adolescence—
we might be labeled Sex Repressive by the experts, even though
we assure our children that sex is good and healthy and fun and
was, in fact, God's idea.

I know some people may laugh at my notion of looking
at women to appreciate God's creativity and would accuse
me of inventing a spiritual reason to leer. I maintain that after
years of steeling myself to avert my eyes from something made
attractive by God, developing an appreciation for it is far
healthier. Clearly it would be wrong to gawk and dwell upon
some stranger's beauty, especially when I have vowed before
God and man to put my wife ahead of all others. Dianna
knows I am attracted to pretty women (she is one, after all).
She also knows that I know they are off-limits and that even
entertaining a lustful thought is wrong. The point is, I don't
pretend before my wife that I no longer look at other women.
My gaze doesn't linger and my thoughts stay in check (not easily and not always), but how much worse it would be if I pretended to have been blind since our wedding and she caught

me sneaking a peek. Her standard line is, "When he quits looking, he quits cooking."

Don't get the idea that my eyes are always roving and that my poor wife can't keep my attention. (Anyone who has seen her knows otherwise.) It doesn't take a lingering look to appreciate beauty, and there are more than enough reasons not to stare at other women. First, it would threaten Dianna and jeopardize my covenant with her. It would be dangerous to my thought life, because past a casual observance of God's handiwork (go ahead, laugh!), my eyes and mind have no right to dwell there. Even if the woman doesn't belong to anyone else, I do!

It's interesting to note the double standard that comes into play here. My glance at a nice-looking woman is even quicker when she's escorted. I know how I feel when men stare at my wife. I watch their eyes. I'm possessive and jealous. I have a right to be. If their gaze lingers, I assume they're trying to catch her eye, and they probably are. No fair. Out of bounds. Off-limits. She's mine. It gives me a great sense of security that Dianna is largely unaware how many heads she turns and that, even if she were aware, she's not one to return another man's gaze. Still, I resent it when I see someone stare at her, and I want to practice the golden rule when the shoe is on the other foot.

I have been quick to point out to my sons that the rush of feeling they might experience for a beautiful woman should never be mistaken for true love. Such a rush is mere infatuation, physical and sensual attraction, a path to a dead end. A relationship may begin with physical attraction, but to build on that alone leads to disaster. It's also important to differentiate here between beauty and cheap sexuality. Almost any woman—within reason—can dress or make herself up in such a way that she looks sexy and available. I maintain that unless a man is looking for thrills, he won't find such a creature attractive. Focusing on a hooker-type is selfish and fleshly, perverting the natural attraction between the sexes that was God's idea.

I realize that women may shake their heads in disgust at my obvious male perspective. Guilty. I was born this way. My friend Lois Mowday covers much the same territory from the female viewpoint in her excellent book *The Snare*,[2] but neither of us could have written the other's book. Men and women think and act differently and are different, and no amount of modern talk can convince me otherwise.

Another high school youth leader first impressed upon me that girls don't think at all like guys do. I didn't believe him at first. Even the minor exposure to pornography a sheltered evangelical male gets tells him that women can be vamps, tramps, teases, flirts, come-ons, hookers, you name it. Therefore, the male assumes that innocent, young Christian girls who dress, act, walk, or talk provocatively know exactly what they are doing. Unless the girls are asking for trouble, which I found difficult to accept, they are playing a dangerous and contemptuous game with us guys. They know we are turned on by hair-trigger switches through the mind and all five senses; so unless they mean business, they are cruel.

This idea that they are, on the whole, ignorant of their effect or unaware how males react was so revelatory and revolutionary that I couldn't accept it. I'm not saying there aren't women base enough to fit precisely the description in the above paragraph, but just that most of those who turn men on would be shocked to know how they are viewed.

I tested that theory as a high school senior and as a college freshman. I dated a Christian girl who was careful and virtuous and could not be described as a flirt. I discussed with her the actions and dress of mutual friends and found that she agreed with our youth leader. The girls in question were ignorant or naive. They were not sinister or on the prowl. I mustered my courage and began to ask them.

My freshman year at a Christian college allowed me to meet many beautiful women students—a whole range of personalities, modes of dress, and behavior. Our school policy stipulated that skirts could be no shorter than the top of the knee. Some of my best friends, women I respected and admired and enjoyed looking at, seemed to push the rule to the limit. How does one determine the top of the knee? (My friends and I volunteered to help!) Depending on the skirt, the material, and the woman, a skirt that was legal while she was standing might be four inches above the knee when she sat. Even the most modest skirt that touched the top of the knee was a problem for men and women when she wanted to cross her legs.

Not wanting to appear an oddball, I waited until I felt a woman was my friend before I popped my question.

"Can I ask you something, just out of curiosity?"

"Sure."

"How would you feel if you thought that the way you dressed caused men to lust?"

I asked at least six college women, ages ranging from eighteen to twenty-one. Every one of them responded with some variation on this answer:

"Oh, I'm sure we don't have any guys that perverted around here."

Remember, I was not on a crusade to get the rule changed or even to get the skirts lengthened. I was just testing a theory, and I was stunned by the response. They actually didn't know. They dressed for fashion, for comfort, and for their own taste. Had they realized they were causing problems for male students, I have no doubt they'd have made adjustments. In fact, things have somehow changed in the ensuing twenty years. I recently read in a Christian college newspaper an editorial by a woman student who said she and her sisters had gotten the point. They felt a responsibility not to lead their brothers into sin. She took it a step further and said some of the guys could take a lesson in how to wear their jeans.

That's a new concept: men turning women on by what they wear and how they wear it. What has contributed to this shift? Some would say novels—written by men that portray women triggered sexually by the same stimuli that affect men, plus the advent of male strippers and magazines like *Playgirl*, which depict male nudity. It is generally accepted that women are aroused by environment, atmosphere, tenderness, romance, and touch. The idea of men baring themselves has been considered repulsive to women. Today you can even see television commercials in which girls on the beach rate the various body parts of the men who walk by. Women friends and relatives tell me, however, that while the occasional broad shoulder or narrow hip might be a mild turn-on, most women are still not sexually aroused in the same way men are. There is no longer any question that women can be aroused to a similar state of excitement and eroticism, but the route is different.[3]

These differences in attraction actually compete with each other. A man is turned on by the mere thought of a beautiful woman—imagining, fantasizing about the possibilities. When he meets a woman, the scenario has already been played out in his mind. She might like his voice, his smile, his manner. Meanwhile, he's light-years ahead. She smiles at his interest. Then he says or does something inappropriate. Immediate disaster. She's turned off, he's offended, and neither understands what went wrong. She thinks he's a typical male. He thinks she's a typical female. Both are right. Some like to blame God for this seeming inequity ("I can't help myself; He made me this way"). Others say that our makeup justifies aggressiveness, that men are to be the leaders, planners, visionaries. Women are to be submissive, supportive, reactive.

Neither view is wholly acceptable, of course. Sure, there are times, especially as teenagers, when we men might wish we hadn't been equipped with an engine that idles like a rocket but that isn't supposed to be launched for years. But to hide behind nature to justify aggression and chauvinism is cowardly. Theologians and psychologists can work out the reasons why we're made this way. Our task is to channel our drives into something positive and to glorify God in the process.

NOTES

1. Miriam Ehrenberg, Ph.D., and Otto Ehrenberg, Ph.D., *The Intimate Circle* (New York: Simon and Schuster, 1988), 47-48.
2. See Lois Mowday, *The Snare* (Colorado Springs, CO: NavPress, 1988).
3. William H. Masters and Virginia E. Johnson, *Human Sexual Response* (Boston: Little, Brown and Co., 1966), 301-302.

4

THE DYNAMICS OF FLIRTATION

Flirting is fun and usually begins in innocence. It's a hard habit to break, even after marriage. Yet it causes jealousy. Worse, it puts us into situations we never intended to fall into, and it creates misunderstandings that can lead to infidelity.

Apart from sex, what could be more fun than flirting? If you say softball, you're reading the wrong book.

Flirting is so much fun because the rushes, emotions, and pleasures are sexual. It's foreplay with no payoff. It makes the heart race, the face flush, and a feeling of well-being wash over the body. It seems harmless, but it's not.

If you want to flirt, flirt with your wife. She may not look, feel, or sound the way she did when you first flirted with her years ago, but she still wants you to flirt with her. Try it. Wink at her across the room. Blow her a kiss no one else sees. Play footsie with her under the table. Give her a squeeze, a pinch, a tickle no one else notices.

Are you afraid she'll think you're crazy? Well, you are crazy, aren't you? Put yourself in her place. Would you like to be flirted with by someone who loves you, someone who can tease about what she might do with you later and then deliver? Do you, or would you, appreciate your wife making a pass at you, making a suggestive comment, giving you a knowing look? I do, and she does, and I love it.

Married couples do not commonly flirt with each other, and the practice may have to be relearned. Marital flirting is really no different than adolescent flirting. You can do the same things, only everything you're thinking about and hoping will come of it is legal, normal, acceptable, and beautiful. Marital flirting is fun and safe.

But . . . who do we usually flirt with? Who would we like to flirt with? Good friends from work? From church? Relatives? Young people? Wives of friends?

We don't mean anything by it. It's innocent. They're safe. It's a way of having a good time at no one else's expense. Right?

Then why does it bother us so much when we detect someone trying to flirt with our wives? A wink, a smile, a "Hey, why don't you dump this guy and run off with me, ha ha," a touch, and the hair on our necks bristles. Who does this guy think he is? He thinks this is funny?

We're also extremely interested in how our wives react to such an approach. Can she bob and weave with the best of them, return the barbs, keep it alive? We trust her. She's faithful. It's all a game, a diversion.

Then why does it bother us so much?

Because the flirter has no right to the emotions, the inappropriate attention, the sexual/recreational lives of our spouses. I don't flirt with other women, even in jest, because I wouldn't want my wife to be offended or hurt or to wonder or be embarrassed. And I certainly would not want her to do the same to me.

My wife doesn't flirt because something deep within her knows it is basically wrong. She doesn't have to fight the urge, and when someone tries to flirt with her, her unpracticed reactions cool his heels. She doesn't try to be mean or cold—though she could be if someone actually came on to her—but extramarital flirtation is so far from her *modus operandi* that she usually doesn't recognize it. Thus her reaction is either puzzlement or seriousness, and a flirt needs a target that flexes, that gives, that bounces back.

Because I enjoy having fun and being funny, and because my mind tends to find humor in words and unusual combinations of ideas, I could easily flirt with anyone I thought was receptive. Much flirting is funny. If someone says something flirtatious to me, my first impulse is to expand on it, play with it, see how quick and funny I can be. But I resist that. It isn't fair. It's mental and emotional unfaithfulness. I would be exercising a portion of my brain and soul reserved for my exclusive lover.

I know that seems rigid, so I am careful not to chastise, put down, or otherwise embarrass or insult a woman who might flatter me by flirting with me. It is flattering, of course, even if it does somehow lower my esteem for her. I usually respond with humor that changes the subject or ends the conversation, in the hope that she will later realize that I deflected the approach without embarrassing her.

The reason I don't scowl at flirters or lecture them is that I believe most flirting is well-intentioned. It's meant to be a compliment, a friendly gesture, a you-and-me kind of thing that separates those of us with certain kinds of minds and attitudes from everyone else in the room. It's elitist. It's subtle. It marks you as smart and clever.

But, as usual, we find ourselves confronted by the age-old difference between men and women. A friend of mine, a woman, says something grossly inappropriate to me almost every time I see her. She does it to bug me, and she has absolutely no ulterior motives. Even my wife thinks she's a scream.

I believe women mean something entirely different by flirting than men do. Most women I have discussed this with tell me that they agree flirting with someone else's husband is not right, and often they feel guilty later. But initiating the flirting or responding to someone else's approach is fun and exciting because of the attention.

"Usually it surprises me," a friend says. "Often a meeting of the eyes or a smile or a flirtatious joke makes me realize for the first time that a man is even aware of me in a group. Then, I admit, I encourage it, but with no thought of actually leading him on."

I'm not saying that men intend anything serious at first either, but if a flirtatious advance is returned, it tends to escalate. I know two men who have left their wives for other men's wives, and it all began with what each party thought was harmless flirting.

In one case, the process took a year; in the other, only a little over a month. In both cases, the same thing happened. The man started it. The woman responded. They teased each other on several occasions until the man grew bold enough to think that maybe she meant something by her encouraging responses. In the first case, he made a move on her; she was stunned and hurt; and in the apologizing and reconciling process, they fell in love. In the second, she was surprised but pleased at his interest, but in the throes of a bad marriage she jumped ship, and two marriages sank.

As with many other innocent activities that eventually get out of hand, flirting can be a good and natural part of a progression toward true love. God made us able to respond emotionally and physically to attention from the opposite sex, and that is the initial aim of flirting. But like any of His gifts, this one can be cheapened and counterfeited and used for evil as well as for good.

I was twelve when I first experienced the euphoric surge of excitement at knowing that a girl and I had locked eyes on purpose. What began as an accident became an anticipated activity. What a revelation! It happened like this:

I helped a friend deliver papers every day. We traded off, from one day to the next, handling the two halves of the territory. One day I tossed a paper onto the big front porch of a house, then moved on. I had just dropped that paper on the steps when I heard the door open and saw a girl about my age come out to retrieve the paper.

I recognized her from school, though I didn't know her— not even her name. She was probably a year ahead of me. As she bent to pick up the paper, her long brown hair cascaded over her face, and as she stood up, she flipped it back into place with a turn of her head. And she looked right at me.

I had been idly watching her as I moved along, but I was embarrassed that she saw me, so I quickly looked elsewhere. But what was that out of the corner of my eye? Had I turned too quickly? Had she smiled at me? I shot a fast double take her way; she had already turned toward the door. But out of the corner of her eye she must have seen me looking back at her, so she turned back.

We smiled shyly at each other and said nothing. I don't know what she was thinking. Probably nothing. To a twelve-year-old, a thirteen-year-old is almost an adult, and I was very much on the young side of twelve. I probably had a ball glove in my newspaper bag, maybe even a pocketful of marbles. My hair would have been flying.

She was more sophisticated. Grown-up. She was probably just smiling at some dumb paperboy, I decided, but I sure liked it. The next day I pleaded with my friend to let me deliver on the same end of the route again. Nothing doing. I would have to wait another twenty-four hours to see that smile. I never considered that it was probably a fluke. Why hadn't I ever seen her before? Did I think she would wait at the window for me next time?

Two days later my hair was combed, my cleanest jeans were on, and I wore new tennies. I imagined her watching from halfway down the block. So I did my best to look older, more conscientious, important, in a hurry, doing a good job. A couple of times I walked past a house without dropping a paper, only to nonchalantly flip one behind my back to the precise spot. I was hot.

At the house before hers I had to mount the steps and put the paper in the rungs under the mailbox. I casually bounded up the stairs two at a time, slipped the paper in, and jumped all the way to the ground. No problem. I don't know what I would have done if I had wound up with a face full of dirt. I imagined her watching, smiling, and I felt like I could do anything. Down deep I was hoping against hope she would come out to get the paper again.

I approached her porch. Slowly. Dropped the paper in front of the door. Turned. More slowly. Then moved resolutely to the next house. No action. No movement. No noise. I looked back several times, hoping. Nothing. Maybe that's why I was doing only one side of the street at a time. When I crossed at the corner and delivered papers to the other side of the same street, I could see her porch for half a block. I worked ever so deliberately.

The house directly across from hers was not that of a paper subscriber, but it sat on a wide expanse of lawn. I delivered the paper to the house before it, then traversed the entire distance to the next with my head turned, staring at the magic porch. Had someone planted a tree in my path the day before, I'd have worn it home. The trail I blazed was as circuitous as you can imagine for one who doesn't have his eye on where he's going.

But my persistence paid off. She appeared. And she wore a fluffy, red dress. She stepped out, picked up the paper, went to the edge of the porch, leaned on the railing, and smiled at me across the street. Her smile and her eyes followed me until I had to look away or careen into the street. This had been no accident. Could she have dressed up just for me? I couldn't swear to it, but clearly she had looked for me, smiled at me, and made it obvious she was pleased to have done so. I began wondering where we might raise our family.

You can't imagine the thrill, unless you remember similar experiences on the threshold of puberty. We continued that ritual every other day for over a week, until I found out she was doing the same to my friend, the other delivery boy. I hadn't even said hello to my intended, and she had already cheated on me. I wasn't even motivated to fight for her. My interest cooled overnight.

As a freshman in high school I enjoyed another silent flirting season with a girl in my algebra class. She was a fresh-faced blonde with glasses and a turned-up nose, and for some reason I loved to look at her. We sat on opposite sides of the room. To see her, I had to lean back and look past all the heads in my row. One day she caught me looking, so I turned back. But when I sneaked another peek, she was staring right at me.

My heart skipped. Was it obvious to everyone that we were in love? I didn't even know her name. Yet my pulse quickened, and I was short of breath when I caught her gaze as I leaned back, and she leaned forward. We didn't even smile at each other. This was too intense. Occasionally I tried to tell myself I was imagining it, and then we would settle into our desks, the teacher would begin, and I would zero in on that pair of eyes.

For a week we stared at each other, sometimes for twenty minutes at a time. I was stunned the teacher did not notice and call us on it. He would not have been able to see both of us staring at the same time, but he could have followed one's gaze to the other.

One day, when I had finally learned her name, I mustered the courage to send a note across to her. Everybody looked at her and then at me as she read it. "See you after class?" it read. She looked up at me, still unsmiling, and nodded. Has there ever been a longer forty-minute wait? I couldn't even look at her that day. I just studied the clock.

After class she went out the door, turned right, stood with her back against the wall and her books embraced in front of her, and waited expectantly. "Hi," I said.

"Hi," she said.

I wanted so badly to say something cool like, "You know, I've really enjoyed studying you these last several days, and I thought it was time we got better acquainted."

But I didn't. I said, "Um, I was wonderin' if you wouldn't mind if I walked you to your next class."

"No problem," she said in a voice too hard, too sharp for such a pretty face. "except it's like right here." She nodded to the study hall next to the algebra room.

"Oh, yeah, well, I guess you can make it there by yourself all right."

"Yeah," she said and walked away.

I saw her again, but I never looked at her, if you know what I mean. I was learning valuable lessons in illusion versus reality.

My point is that the same surge of ecstasy is still available to me—or to any man—today. If you work at it, you can catch a woman's eye and see if she wants to play the game. The problem is that it's short of adultery only in the physical sense, and it can lead to that.

I'm sometimes embarrassed in public, maybe in a restaurant, when I happen to catch the gaze of a woman, look away, and then we look back at the same moment. Neither of us is looking for anything; each is embarrassed and wonders what the other thinks. I usually smile apologetically and then fight the urge to look once more.

I'm not looking for other women's eyes, and I don't want them or anyone, especially my wife, to think that I am. There is a comfort, a sensuality, a sexuality, a bonding deeper than with anyone else when I look deeply into Dianna's eyes. I know her, I can read her, and we can communicate that way.

On the occasion of his and Ruth's sixtieth wedding anniversary, Dr. Billy Graham told me, "We realize that at this stage of our lives [both in their mid-eighties and failing physically], we can continue our love affair with our eyes."

Besides looking, I also flirt with Dianna by touching, caressing, yes, even playing footsie. We consider these fun and funny personal and private ways of communicating. They make up a part of our sexual language of love, and every one of them—the looks, smiles, and suggestive comments—are off-limits for anyone else.

I don't flirt with anyone but my wife, and vice versa.

You flirt with your wife, and I'll flirt with mine.

5

THE BIBLICAL BASIS FOR HEDGES

People will tell you to beware of legalism, even in the area of sexual purity. True, a balanced, appropriate view makes our stand attractive rather than shrill. But Scripture is clear: There's a price for adultery.

We're far enough along now that the following should be no revelation: I'm assuming you care what God thinks about your life. If you don't, you're reading the wrong book. I believe in God, and I accept the Bible as the basis of authority for my life. If you don't, this has all long since appeared foolish to you anyway.

Perhaps you're in the middle on these issues. Maybe you aren't sure about a personal God and are very unsure whether the Bible is relevant. That puts you in the same category, sadly, as many who call themselves Christians. They are smorgasbord church people who sample what looks good and leave what doesn't. A God who cares about sexual conduct and even has rules regarding it doesn't fit contemporary me-first society.

The problem with that view is that it assumes God has rules for rules' sake. He's just a spoilsport, trying to make a goody-two-shoes out of everybody. If we can't find practical reasons for following His rules, we justify ignoring them.

My simple mind cries out for a God who is personal, orderly, and logical. I believe that a God who created everything and loved us enough to make the supreme sacrifice for us has reasons for His prohibitions and would rather see us happy and fulfilled than miserable and confined.

There must be sense and logic behind His rules. Let's look at them briefly to determine what they are, and then let me make an amateur's—or at least a layman's—attempt at making them fit with my view of God as a fulfiller, not a taskmaster.

HERE COMES THE JUDGE

Jesus talks about the law most extensively in Matthew 5:17-19:

> Do not think that I came to destroy the Law or the Prophets. I did not come to destroy but to fulfill. For assuredly, I say to you, till heaven and earth pass away, one jot or one tittle will by no means pass from the law till all is fulfilled. Whoever therefore breaks one of the least of these commandments, and teaches men so, shall be called least in the kingdom of heaven; but whoever does and teaches them, he shall be called great in the kingdom of heaven.

The law He's talking about, of course, is the Ten Commandments. Most people, even non-churchgoers, can remember a few of them. Don't lie, don't murder, don't commit adultery, don't steal. We can see the obvious problems with lying, stealing, and murdering, but if sex is so good and beautiful and fun, what's wrong with a little adultery among friends?

And what is Jesus talking about when He says He's fulfilling, not replacing, the law? This is the wrong forum from which to get into Jesus' claims of deity, but suffice it to say He was establishing Himself as one with God, the Son of God, the fulfillment of God's law. The embodiment of perfection, the personification of sinlessness—that was Jesus Christ. Now—lest anyone else claim to also qualify as the righteous king—Jesus, in essence, changes all the rules.

Later in the same discourse He says,

> Unless your righteousness exceeds the righteousness of the scribes and Pharisees, you will by no means enter the kingdom of heaven. You have heard that it was said to those of old, "You shall not murder, and whoever murders will be in danger of the judgment." But I say to you that whoever is angry with his brother without a cause shall be in danger of the judgment. (vv. 20-22a)

Murder is worthy of judgment, but now even anger with a brother is just as bad. Who can live up to that standard? Only Jesus. Then He gets down to the toughest part. "You have heard that it was said to those of old, 'You shall not commit adultery.' But I say to you that whoever looks at a woman to lust for her has already committed adultery with her in his heart" (vv. 27-28).

What is the point of all that? Wasn't the original law hard enough? Wasn't it a good enough standard by which to be judged? Why would Jesus rewrite it to make it impossible? Let me speculate, as a layman. Jesus, the God/man who died for us, could take no pleasure in making life difficult or unachievable for us. Clearly he was setting a standard to make a point—that if someone was somehow able to keep from lying, murdering, even coveting for an entire lifetime, there was no way to ever dream of following this new standard. If hatred and anger equal murder, and lust is adultery, we're all guilty.

Only Jesus could meet that standard; so we are forced to rely upon Him for our standing before God. He takes the penalty for our sin; He becomes our advocate before a holy God. God looks at us and sees not our sin but the perfection of Jesus, and we who would otherwise be unqualified to be in His presence are assured of a place with Him for eternity. The apostle Paul said it this way in 2 Corinthians 5:21: "For He made Him who knew no sin to be sin for us, that we might become the righteousness of God in Him."

BETWEEN OUR EARS

When my friend Robert Wolgemuth teaches from Matthew, he makes the point that Jesus is not really talking about murder or adultery but about attitudes, what goes on between our ears. Jesus is talking about the things most people can't see. Jesus is saying that the law is not about something you do or don't do; it's about something you are.

The question then arises as to why Jesus puts adultery in the same category as murder. Leviticus 20:10 says, "The man who commits adultery with another man's wife, he who commits adultery with his neighbor's wife, the adulterer and the adulteress, shall surely be put to death." Murderers and adulterers deserve death according to the law, and Jesus has made the law impossible to obey. What's going on?

A lot of this, I admit, is not comprehensible this side of heaven, but we had better find out why these two sins are considered equally reprehensible before we start building our lives on our own principles. Why was it so important that people not commit adultery? I submit that the reasons, whatever they are, are the same reasons we need to plant hedges around our hearts, eyes, hands, spouses, and marriages. If adultery is in the same class as murder, it is a threat not only to our marriages but to our very lives.

Some have said that only a crazy person can commit murder. A man or woman has to lose contact with reality to become so angry or distraught or jealous that he or she can take another's life. I've found that adulterers suffer this same malady. They violate a vow they made years before, drag their wife and family through torture and disgrace, and set aside or reformat their entire set of values. How else could a man justify the chaos wrought by his actions?

A friend of mine once found himself pulled into a situation in which he was to officiate at a family meeting where an adulterous father tried to explain to his children, in front of his wife, why he was leaving her for another woman. One of this man's first assertions was that he had never really loved his wife. (To a person who believes that love is a feeling rather than an act of the will, falling out of love or deciding you never loved someone is a convenient rationalization.)

The teenage son said, "How, after all these years, can you say you don't love Mom? After all we've done together . . ."

The only way the man could live with himself was to tell himself lies, to reorder his standards. He said to his younger daughter, "Honey, tell me what you're thinking."

She looked up at him, fighting for composure. "I'm thinking I'm sad."

ADULTERY CAUSES CHAOS

Adulterers are liars, and they are as good at it as alcoholics are. Another friend of mine was awakened in the middle of the night by a call informing him of the infidelity of a good friend. He didn't believe it, so he went to see the man. "Dave," he said, "what's the story about you and this woman?"

Dave played dumb. "It's not true," he said, looking my friend squarely in the eye. "No way. Not me. Never have, never will."

"Wait a minute," my friend said. "What about all these allegations?" He proceeded with a litany of charges, names, dates, places.

"Someone's trying to frame me," Dave said. "Never happened."

What a relief! My friend wouldn't have to see this man confess to his wife, disappoint her, break her heart, ruin their marriage. It was good news.

Good news until two months later when my friend's wife got a call from Dave's wife. She was hysterical. My friend and his wife raced to her home while Dave was away on business. She had discovered the affair and had a pile of evidence to prove it. My friend was assigned to meet Dave at the airport upon his return. Rather than being met by his family as usual, Dave was puzzled to see my friend standing there solemnly. "It's over," my friend told him. "Your wife knows, and I know."

He led Dave to the parking lot where his car was jammed floor to ceiling with his belongings. There was barely room for the two men. Dave drove my friend home and then set out to look for a place to live. My friend watched him pull out of sight in the darkness, and he knew: Adultery causes chaos.

An acquaintance once told me that, yes, he had been seeing another woman, but, no, he was not interested in her romantically and didn't think she was interested in him either.

They were just friends. Middle of the night, sometimes all-night friends. He liked her baby daughter. Yeah, that was it. They had a lot in common, talked easily, liked each other's company. I told him he didn't have the right to have a woman as a close friend when he was married and that it was slowly killing his wife.

He seemed to see the light and said he would break it off that night, and I returned to his wife with the wonderful news. That night he met the woman after work. I saw them embrace and kiss before they left the state in her car. By the time he really came to his senses and pleaded for his wife to take him back—he missed his four boys terribly—the divorce was final.

Adultery causes chaos.

ARE YOU GUILTY?

As much as television, movies, and videos try to convince us otherwise, adultery is not funny. The media have convinced too many people that adultery is no more serious than exceeding the speed limit. "Everybody does it." "This is a new age." "Don't be so old-fashioned." "Get with the program." You can hardly watch a current sitcom without illicit sex as part of the story.

If the Bible deals with this modern issue, it had better do it in a sophisticated, up-to-date way or no one will pay any attention. What could a musty old religious tome have to say about life as we know it today?

Remember Leviticus 20:10? Adulterers are put to death.

Remember Matthew 5:27-28? Lust is adultery.

Are you guilty?

You may be guilty of more than lust. You may be guilty of adultery itself, and more than once. Be glad Jesus fulfilled the law for you, because even if your offense was the attitude and not the act, you are still guilty.

But there is forgiveness. There is starting over. There is a future for you. John 8:3-11 tells this story:

> Then the scribes and Pharisees brought to Him a woman caught in adultery. And when they had set her in the midst, they said to Him, "Teacher, this woman was caught in adultery, in the very act. Now Moses, in the law, commanded us that such should be stoned. But what do You say?" This they said, testing Him, that they might have something of which to accuse Him.
>
> But Jesus stooped down and wrote on the ground with His finger, as though He did not hear. So when they continued asking Him, He raised Himself up and said to them, "He who is without sin among you, let him throw a stone at her first." And again He stooped down and wrote on the ground.
>
> Then those who heard it, being convicted by their conscience, went out one by one, beginning with the oldest even to the last. And Jesus was left alone, and the woman standing in the midst. When Jesus had raised Himself up and saw no one but the woman, He said to her, "Woman, where are those accusers of yours? Has no one condemned you?"
>
> She said, "No one, Lord."
>
> And Jesus said to her, "Neither do I condemn you; go and sin no more."

Don't make the mistake of assuming that Jesus was condoning adultery. He called her adultery sin and told her to "*sin no more.*" I've always appreciated the irony in this story. Jesus says that the one "among you" without sin should cast the first stone. Have you ever thought about the fact that there *was* one among them who was without sin? It was Jesus Himself. And He chose not to cast a stone. His point was to label the accusers as adulterers, because indeed we all are— even if we have never committed the act. We may not have murdered, but we have hated; and we may not have committed adultery, but we have lusted. And Jesus says to us with the voice of loving forgiveness that rings through the ages, "Neither do I condemn you; go and sin no more."

Out of pure thanks and appreciation and wonder at that freeing compassion, we should want to obey.

BUT WHAT ABOUT TEMPTATION?

First Corinthians 10:13 says, "No temptation has overtaken you except such as is common to man; but God is faithful, who will not allow you to be tempted beyond what you are able, but with the temptation will also make the way of escape, that you may be able to bear it."

The problem with lust and its result is that it is difficult to resist and that people try everything to win over it. They pray, they stand and fight, they resolve, when all the while our plan of attack is clear—and it's not a plan of attack at all. We are to retreat! Paul wrote to his young friend in 2 Timothy 2:22, "Flee also youthful lusts; but pursue righteousness, faith, love, peace with those who call on the Lord out of a pure heart."

The problem with the temptation verse (1 Corinthians 10:13) is that people apply it too late. Ten minutes into foreplay with the wrong partner, they're ready to seek that way of escape that was supposed to have come with the temptation. That's just it: The escape comes with the temptation. It's preventive medicine, not first aid after you've already set your course on a path toward injury.

MORE BIBLICAL BASES FOR HEDGES

Need more evidence that there are biblical bases for planting hedges around your marriage? Psalm 89:40 implies that strongholds are brought to ruin when hedges are broken down. Job 1:10 implies that Job was so richly blessed—before God allowed him to be tested—because God had "made a hedge around him, around his household, and around all that he ha[d] on every side."

Jesus told parables about landowners who planted vineyards and protected them with hedges. When those hedges were trampled or removed, ruin came to the precious possessions of the landowners.

We hold people and relationships much more precious than land or holdings. If we can keep from deceiving ourselves about our own resolve and inner strength, we will see the necessity for a healthy row of blossoming hedges that keep love in and infidelity out.

THE POWER OF
SELF-DECEPTION

Knowing our own weakness is one way to begin tilling the soil for the seeds that will grow the hedges that will protect us.

Before I get into my own list of hedges, which evidences also my own weaknesses, I need to ask: What are yours?

A friend of mine has planted two hedges for his business life. First, he stays away from pornography, which is becoming more difficult all the time, given the illusion of privacy via the Internet and the pervasiveness of what is piped into almost every hotel room in the world.

Rather than pretend to be disgusted and turned off by it, he admits porn can be seductive. It can be tantalizing. Although looking at pornography may result in disgust with himself and wondering how he could ever be attracted to such a cheapening of God's gift of sexuality, he is more successful in fending it off by acknowledging in advance that it's something he wants to avoid.

In hotels he tells the front desk to lock it out. Sometimes

the clerk will act surprised or wonder aloud if he has children with him in spite of his reservation as a single. (I've told desk clerks, "Yes, there's a kid here. It's the big one talking to you right now.") My friend clarifies he is alone and insists on the lock-out service. As part of this hedge he often travels with a business partner, and they keep each other honest.

What if my friend told himself that since he had gone many years without succumbing to the temptation of pornography, he could surely travel on his own and not have to embarrass himself by asking a desk clerk half his age to lock out the adult movies? A sexy show on regular television might whet his appetite for something racier, something he might not even consider if he did not know it was available. But with the seemingly innocuous touch of a button, with the first five minutes not even billed to his room (and no titles appearing on his bill if he does wind up paying for it), he might convince himself he's mature enough to satisfy his curiosity.

The key is preventive maintenance. Once that first step has been taken down the road of self-deceit and rationalization, there is no turning back. Each excuse sounds more plausible, and before he knows it, the typical male has satisfied every curiosity, every urge. Regardless of the remorse, the self-loathing, and the pledges, the pattern will repeat itself for as long as he refuses to flee. There is no other defense.

Many hotel systems allow for the viewer himself to lock out the channels. Take advantage of this, but plan ahead. Do it before you sit down, before you unpack. Just flip on the set, find the mechanism to lock out the adult channels for the length of your stay, and hit it before you start talking yourself out of it.

My friend's second hedge comes in the form of pictures

of his wife and his two daughters that he carries in his wallet. These pictures serve the usual function of reminding him of his loved ones and allowing him to brag about his beautiful family. But they also serve as a safety net, which he used several years ago when he found himself next to a beautiful, young, single woman on an airplane.

Normally he feigns fatigue and isn't interested in conversing during a long flight, but this woman was fun to look at and more fun to talk to. He asked her about herself. She sounded more interesting and exciting every minute. She was staying in the same city for which he was headed. She had a car and could give him a ride to his hotel. And why not? Each seemed nice enough to the other.

WE'RE NOT ALL THE SAME

To illustrate differences in styles and personalities, I must say that I would have hidden behind a hedge I planted years ago that does not allow me to accept a ride alone with an unrelated woman. I wouldn't trust my weak, self-deceiving, rationalizing mind once I was alone with a beautiful, willing female. My friend, however, used a different hedge and was able to accept the ride. When she asked about him, he pulled out his wallet. Before he showed her the photos of his wife and daughters, he looked at them himself.

"It was as if they spoke to me right out of that wallet," he says. "They said, 'Thanks, Daddy, for being faithful to Mom and to us.'"

He smiled as he showed her the pictures and spoke lovingly of his family, especially of his wife, Jackie. The conversation mellowed and became friendly in a different sort of way than before. My friend rode with the woman to his hotel, shook her hand, and heard her say in farewell, "Say hi to Jackie for me."

"If you think I didn't want to spend the night with her," he says, "you're crazy."

But it sure wasn't worth his spiritual, mental, and family life. He used a hedge, one that wouldn't have worked for me, but one effective for him and his personality.

CUSTOM-MAKE YOUR HEDGES

Just as my friend used a different hedge than I would have, so there are also temptations difficult for some and not for others. For instance, the temptation to frequent prostitutes happens to be one I can only write about and not identify with. I know it's a very real temptation and that it has been "the ruin of many a poor boy." I know this temptation is one that has been the ruin of Christians, even preachers, and that the book of Proverbs is replete with admonitions about and against it. It just happens, though, that this is an area in which I have never been tempted—although I was propositioned once.

I was on business in Cleveland and had unknowingly booked a hotel room in the seediest part of town. The hotel chain was large and well-known. So I was stunned when I went out for a walk and found myself in the red-light district. While I might have been young and curious enough to be tempted to slip into an adult movie theater, my fear of a fire bomb or a raid was sufficient defense. "Christian Writer Among Dead in Adult Theater Fire" would have been a nice final page for my wife's scrapbook, eh? Fear of detection is not the most altruistic motive for avoiding such temptations, but use whatever works at the point of weakness.

It was dark, and the area seemed overrun with potential muggers. I was hurrying back to my hotel when a teenaged hooker made me an offer I'm sure she thought I couldn't refuse. I was nearly paralyzed. I had always wondered what I would say. This girl was not unattractive, but I had not the slightest second thought. The question was what I would say.

I could have ignored her and kept walking, which I would do today. I could have looked shocked and disgusted and told her off. I could have witnessed to her. (I have friends who do that, but I don't recommend it unless you're with your wife or a group. Say the wrong thing while witnessing to an undercover cop and you'll find yourself, and your ministry, in the overnight lockup. Or, if you're alone, try explaining to someone who recognizes you just what you were saying to the hooker on the corner.)

Well, I was in my early twenties, and all my upbringing and training came to the fore. I was polite, maddeningly, and as I think about it, hilariously polite. I said, "No, thanks."

She looked disappointed. "Are you sure?"

"Yes, but thanks anyway."

"What you wanna be alone for tonight when you can be indulgin' yourself?"

"That's all right," I said. "I hope you won't be offended if I pass."

As she shrugged and trudged on, I thought, *I hope you won't be offended? What a stupid thing to say!* That girl was threatening my moral and spiritual health, trying to get me to jeopardize my marriage, encouraging me to go against everything I had ever been taught or believed, and I was polite!

ARE YOU LONESOME TONIGHT?

I was with an older colleague in a top-flight hotel in Detroit several years ago when we smelled perfume and heard a spraying sound near the door. He tiptoed over in stocking feet to discover that indeed someone was spraying perfume under the door. He swung the door open to see a ghastly middle-aged woman in a miniskirt leaning seductively in the frame.

"You lonely, hon?" she said.

"I'll never be that lonely," he said and shut the door. I wish I'd thought of that.

On the other hand, I heard a prominent preacher say that he got on an elevator in a hotel in a big city and was greeted warmly by two beautiful young women. A glib, social type, he engaged them in friendly banter before they boldly asked him to join them in their room. "In the space of less than a minute, I had to make a decision," he says. "I was far from home. I could get away with this, in one sense." He knew it would be wrong, silently prayed for the strength to resist, and left the elevator on his own floor.

It can be disappointing to hear that a man of God would have to talk himself out of something like that, but each man carries with him his own weaknesses and temptations. Whereas I have never been able even to imagine being attracted to or turned on by a woman who has had sex with others all day, I do plant hedges against being alone or working too closely with women I simply admire or like. That, to me, is more dangerous. I could see myself becoming attached to or enamored with someone I worked with if I didn't emphasize keeping everything on a professional basis.

A WORD OF CAUTION

Just because I cannot imagine ever being tempted by a prostitute doesn't mean I am cavalier or naive about their areas and haunts. There are other forms of illegal activity that don't tempt me either, but I don't hang around their headquarters.

In other words, if you're tempted to cruise prostitution row, the way of escape is to do something else. Go somewhere else. While you have your wits about you—before you're at the edge of the abyss—set a rule for yourself that you won't drive within a certain number of blocks of the area for any reason.

Some hedges may appear ridiculous to you because they are unnecessary in your life—just like the one above is for me. I used to drive home right through an area where hookers frequented the corners. I knew enough not to look interested, because I truly wasn't. I was curious, sure, wondering about these sad girls with wasted bodies and faces, clearly addicted to drugs, waving at cars and trying to avoid detection by police. But tempting it was not.

A man I used to work with told me he drove through that area, and as he was looking at a hooker while at a stoplight, she approached his car. She asked if he wanted a date. He said no, but she seemed friendly; so he asked her what the going rate was for a date. She told him. He smiled at her, waved, and drove off. I knew him. He would not have been any more attracted to a prostitute than I was, but he had been stupid. Somehow, even with the spate of documentaries and dramas about the world of prostitution, he had missed that negotiating the price is the operative offense that can get you locked up. Had his hooker been an undercover cop, he would have been arrested for negotiating with a prostitute.

STUPIDITY

Too many men are stupid in other ways. They think they can handle any temptation. Their resolve, their marriage, their spirituality will carry the day. These men are self-deceived, and we all know too many of them.

No one wants to admit he has a problem or a weakness. I confess it bothered me when I heard the minister in the hotel elevator story above give that account. I wondered why he didn't admit to some other, less offensive temptation, like maybe the urge to spend more on a car than he should have. For some reason we don't want our spiritual heroes to be human. Wives don't want their husbands to be human. Kids don't want their dads to be human. We'd all like to know someone who is so spiritual, so wise, so disciplined that he could ignore or throw away a men's magazine left in his hotel room by the previous guest. I'll tell you, if I didn't throw it out upon first discovering it, ignoring it would be a chore.

No one likes to admit that. I can hear people saying, "How disgusting! Who would want to poison his mind with that trash?"

Certainly not I. Or would I? All I know to do, according to Paul's letter to Timothy, is to flee. Why? Because of what Paul also says in his letter to the Romans:

> For what I am doing, I do not understand. For what I will to do, that I do not practice; but what I hate, that I do. If, then, I do what I will not to do, I agree with the law that it is good. But now, it is no longer I who do it, but sin that dwells in me. For I know that in me (that is, in my flesh) nothing good dwells; for to will is present with me, but how to perform what is good I do not find. (7:15-18)

And in Romans 7:22-25 Paul tells us:

For I delight in the law of God according to the inward man. But I see another law in my members, warring against the law of my mind, and bringing me into captivity to the law of sin which is in my members. O wretched man that I am! Who will deliver me from this body of death? I thank God—through Jesus Christ our Lord! So then, with the mind I myself serve the law of God, but with the flesh the law of sin.

The only future in self-deceit is ruin. Let's quit kidding ourselves. No, we don't have to broadcast every base thought and urge to the public, but in our heart of hearts, let's avoid denial. If the greatest missionary in the history of Christendom could make himself vulnerable by admitting that in his flesh dwells no good thing, who are we to think we should be above carnal drives and desires?

The only regret I have since going on my hedges campaign a few years ago is that occasionally some wonderful woman colleague or new friend will say, "I don't know how to act around you, whether I can touch you or not, or even shake your hand."

The last thing I want is a reputation as a guy who is desperately trying to contain his lustful thoughts for everything in a skirt. As you'll see later, I do trust myself to touch and even embrace women I'm not related to. But I have strict guidelines and hedges because I do not want to fall to my own self-deceit.

Let's start planting some practical hedges.

PART TWO

HOW TO START PLANTING

*Here are pragmatic ways to guard
ourselves against our weaknesses.
We can plant hedges only after we have
determined where they must grow.*

7

TWO'S COMPANY; THREE'S SECURITY

Hedge No. 1—Whenever I need to meet or dine or travel with an unrelated woman, I make it a threesome. Should an unavoidable last-minute complication make this impossible, my wife hears it from me first.

This hedge is about pure logic. Scripture is clear that Christians should "abstain from sexual immorality" (1 Thessalonians 4:3), for "this is the will of God."

So, you ask, what is sexually immoral about meeting, dining, or traveling with an unrelated woman? Nothing. But it is also true that, unless I am alone with a woman, I will not engage in immorality with her.

But, you're still wondering, what does one necessarily have to do with the other? In other words, if it is true that I won't commit adultery if I'm not alone with a woman, is it also true that if I am alone with her, I will? No, that is not logical. Logic says that if I am following the biblical injunction to abstain from even the "appearance of evil"

(1 Thessalonians 5:22, KJV), I will also abstain from the evil itself.

My philosophy is that if you take care of how things look, you take care of how they are.

I once worked in a building where we had a tiny window in every office door. When these were installed forty or fifty years ago, they were not intended to make immorality difficult. They were intended to eliminate suspicion and protect reputations. As long as that little eye to the outside world is uncovered, no one feels free to attempt anything untoward, and just as importantly, no one else is suspicious about what goes on behind closed doors. Were it not for those little windows, I would have felt obligated to invite my secretary to every brief meeting I had with a woman or to keep my door open.

Why? Am I really that weak or dangerous? Or are those with whom I might meet? No, I don't think so. But I don't want the reputations of the woman, my employer, my wife, or my Lord—not to mention myself—even questioned.

RISKY BUSINESS

One of the saddest and scariest stories I've ever heard on this subject was about a young evangelist. He was just twenty-one, on fire for God, effective in his preaching and soul-winning, and in great demand from local churches. He had preached several large crusades and was soon invited to an area-wide effort at which he would be the main speaker.

Though he was not yet even out of college, he was a protégé of international evangelist Sammy Tippit and was admired and considered wise. Though he didn't have a steady girlfriend, he dated regularly at Bible college. Spiritually he was alert and mature. He was, however, naive. The first night of the crusade he supervised the counseling ministry in a large room near the pastor's study. A beautiful teenager asked if she could speak with him personally. He tried to assign her to someone else, but when she persisted, he agreed she could wait until he was finished with the others.

More than an hour after the meeting had ended, the rest of the counselors and counselees had left, and he was alone with the young girl. A few minutes later she burst from the room, screaming, "He made a pass at me! He wanted to make love to me!"

That very night the pastor of the host church and a small group of the crusade planners confronted the young preacher and demanded an explanation. He denied the girl's charge but had no witnesses. The girl had seemed an upstanding young woman in the church, and there was no reason to disbelieve her.

"What did happen in that room?" the pastor demanded.

"To tell you that would be to make an accusation behind someone's back," he said. "Which is what happened to me. I ask only that I be allowed to face my accuser." The pastor and the others canceled the rest of the crusade and agreed that the young woman should be asked to face the preacher in their presence. Two nights later she showed up with her parents at a private board meeting. The pastor asked if she would care to speak about her charges against the preacher.

"She has already said all she has to say," her father said sternly, her mother nodding and glaring at the accused.

"Would you, son, care to share your version of what happened?"

"No, sir," the evangelist said. "I see no future in that. Only she and I know the truth, and I cannot defend myself. I'd just like to say this to her. Cindy, you know what happened and what didn't happen in that room. If you don't tell the truth, I will be branded and may never preach again. This will damage my reputation and that of this church and even that of God. If I did what you say I did, I deserve no better, but we both know that is not the truth. I'm begging you in the name of Christ to set the record straight."

The silence hung heavy as the board and her parents watched her face contort until the tears began to flow. "I lied," she said quietly. "I'm sorry. I lied. He didn't make a pass at me; I made a pass at him. When he turned me down, I was so embarrassed and ashamed and angry that I made up that story. I'm so sorry!"

Had that young evangelist not had the wisdom to face his accuser in just that manner, his ministry might have been ruined forever. And had not God worked in that young girl's heart, she might have sat there silently, refusing to change her story.

That preacher is no longer young. He has never again allowed himself to be alone in a room with a female to whom he is not related. Along with his spiritual wisdom came a painful, almost fatal farewell to naiveté. He might have been embarrassed that night, early in his ministry, if he'd had to ask someone to stay with him while he counseled the young woman, or if he'd had to tell her that he could see her only in the sanctuary. But now he sees embarrassment, or sometimes even the risk of offending, a small price for the protection of all those reputations.

A MOVABLE FEAST

You may have noticed that I included dining alone with my meeting and traveling prohibitions. I don't know why, but there is something very personal and even intimate about eating with someone. If that weren't true, why are so many dates centered on food?

My embargo against dining alone with an unrelated woman is also for my wife's sake. Dianna is not the jealous type, but this way I don't have to keep track of every lunch partner so I can tell her about each one before someone else does. People love to say, "Oh, I saw your husband having lunch with so-and-so the other day," with that lilt in their voice that begs to know if anything is going on.

My intention is that if someone told Dianna that I had been seen with someone alone, she would immediately say, "No, he wasn't" because she knows if that were to happen, she would have known about it first. Once my secretary and I invited a friend of hers to have lunch with us. At the last minute the friend was unable to go. We just changed our plans, had the lunch delivered, and enjoyed it in the office with the door open. I mentioned it to my wife in advance, as a courtesy.

The first few times my secretary and I changed our plans because a third party was unavailable, she may have thought I was being ridiculous. She had no designs on me, and vice versa, though we were friends. I'm sure I seemed to be straining at a gnat. But over the years, as we saw marriage after marriage fail and family after family suffer, my prudish rules made more sense.

There will always be times, of course, when rules cannot be followed to the letter. During my years as an executive in Chicago I occasionally found it necessary to drop a woman colleague off at one office building or another. Sometimes this came up when it was inconvenient or impossible to let my wife know in advance. It would have been silly to wait until I could either tell her or ask permission. I told her later, and though she never demanded it, she always appreciated it. On those rare occasions when I did question the reputation of one with whom I might have to meet or dine or travel alone, I didn't think twice. I didn't call to inform Dianna or to ask her permission. I just didn't go.

ON THE ROAD

Travel is chock-full of dangerous possibilities for appearances and behavior. Assume that every motive is pure. How does it look for a man and a woman who don't belong to each other to be on a long trip together—in a car, on a plane, in a cab, at the same hotel, even if in separate rooms?

I had to travel to a distant city with a woman manager who reported to me; so I asked her to select someone to go with us. The young woman she chose woke up ill on departure day, and I didn't learn about it until I arrived at the airport. My manager was also a friend of our family, which helped, and though she was single and close to my age, our relationship was such that we didn't worry about anything happening. We worried most about how the trip would look.

Because originally she had planned to room with the younger woman, we had thought nothing of booking our seats together on the plane and sharing a ride to—and staying at— the same hotel. All those arrangements had been made, but I was willing to absorb the cost of canceling them if necessary. My first query was to the manager herself. She expressed her knowledge of, trust in, and respect for me; she said she had no problem traveling with me, but that she would understand if I chose not to go.

I then called my boss. An unwritten rule in our ministry forbade unrelated men and women traveling together without a third party, but under the circumstances my boss left it up to me. With a phone call from the airport, I passed the buck to my wife. She nearly laughed. The fact that I had called her and had made a practice of keeping her informed of such seeming improprieties for years gave her the confidence to immediately agree to the trip.

ADVICE FROM ONE WHO KNOWS

In *Advance* magazine,[1] evangelist Robert M. Abbott writes that just as the fact that "a certain percentage of people die annually through traffic accidents does not mean we stop searching for ways to remedy the situation," neither should we be ready to shrug off moral impurity among our leaders.

Abbott continues, "None of us plan[s] to have moral accidents, but we must also plan not to! Danger rides with us all the time." He compares the moral danger to that of a driver pulling several tons of equipment behind his car. "[This] requires more braking power and a longer stopping time. . . . Brakes! Thank God for brakes!"

Abbott writes that "[we] must learn to keep plenty of space between us and sinful acts, so we can start braking soon enough to stop before it is too late." He offers a list of twenty-eight times when we might "need to put on the brakes early and well." Among them:

• When you are so busy there is no time to be alone with God.

• When you are too busy to spend at least one relaxed evening a week with your wife and family.

• When you feel you deserve more attention than you are getting at home.

• When you wouldn't want your wife or colleagues to see what you are reading or looking at.

• When the romance in your marriage is fading.

• When your charisma, appearance, and personality are attractive to women and you are tempted to make the most of it.

• When you enjoy fantasizing about an illicit relationship.

• When a woman makes herself available by her behavior.

• When some woman tells you how wonderful you are and how much she loves you.

• When [you think] Scriptures concerning adultery are for others, not you.

• When you start feeling sorry for yourself.

• When you hope God isn't looking or listening.

Sadly, many pastors and other Christian leaders fall into sexual temptation because of a common problem. They have planted no hedges and find themselves counseling weeping, exasperated women who seem to have a lot to offer but are frustrated in bad marriages. They wish their husbands were more spiritual, more popular, had more leadership qualities, were more authoritative, more patient, better listeners, men of the Word, men of prayer.

And guess what? The pastor fills the bill on every point. The woman may be surprised to find herself falling for him, but once she has, she'll find the fact difficult to hide. And the pastor may at first innocently enjoy being so revered by a woman who needs him. If his wife is nagging him for spending too much time at church, he may begin looking forward to private counseling sessions with a woman who worships him, eats out of his hand, and gives him her full attention.

Pastors and other Christian leaders need hedges as much, if not more, than the rest of us. If they counsel women at all—and they would, in most cases, do better to assign them to some wise, older women in the church—they should counsel with the door open and the secretary close by. Meetings with any female staff member or parishioner should take place only in public or with at least one other person there.

The dining and traveling hedges should never be trampled when it comes to pastors being with unrelated women. And the only reason their standards are stricter than for us rank-and-file types is that, in most cases, more is at stake.

For all of us, however, the price of suspicion is high, and the price of infidelity is even higher. There are more hedges to plant.

NOTES

1. Robert M. Abbott, "Thank God for Brakes," *Advance*, July 1985.

8

TOUCHY, TOUCHY!

Hedge No. 2—I am careful about touching. While I might shake hands or squeeze an arm or a shoulder in greeting, I embrace only dear friends or relatives, and only in front of others.

I don't know when touching returned to vogue in the United States, but I recall clearly when the encounter group, get-in-touch-with-yourself philosophy finally reached the church. I was in high school in the mid-sixties, and somewhere around that time something new began.

Worship became more expressive. People became more emotional. And maybe because there was a significant Jesus People movement heading east from California, and that movement had originated among street people and hippies accustomed to more openness than the rest of society, certain things became more acceptable in the church.

It wasn't all bad. I was visiting a camp when I was about fifteen, and after a particularly moving evening of testimonies, singing, and speaking, people were weeping and swaying as they sang with arms around each other's shoulders.

That was interesting and different, but what impressed me was the freedom everyone felt after that to hug each other. I had a girlfriend I didn't mind hugging, but I wasn't crazy about anyone else hugging her. I was shocked to see high school girls hugging camp leaders I knew were married, but it didn't seem to bother anyone else.

That was at a time of life when I would have enjoyed hugging any female, but still it didn't seem right. At that age you wonder if you can control yourself if given the opportunity to embrace a beautiful girl. Suddenly it seemed okay to hug anybody who was as happy as you were because we were brother and sister in Christ.

I was slow to catch onto the joy of it, and it was hard to keep emotions and feelings in check when you could embrace an adult woman, plus all the girls your own age. It happened all of a sudden, this new freedom, and there was something spiritual about it.

The rub (pardon the pun) was that—unless I was the only pervert around—I had a good idea that most of the guys my age were less spiritual and more sensual and physical about all this, regardless of their high ideals. And we all did have high ideals. As I mentioned in Chapter 2, one of my deepest desires was to remain sexually pure—celibate, virginal—before marriage. This I did, with God's (and a chaste girlfriend's) help, but, I confess, this new wrinkle in social behavior was of little assistance.

Say I was a hot-blooded teenager if you want, but this new openness to embrace was both a dream come true and a nightmare for the two sides of my nature. Christian psychologist James Dobson says that outside of hunger, the most powerful of all the human urges is the sexual appetite. He adds that Christians have the same biochemical forces within their bodies that non-Christians do, and I can add from experience that teenagers, especially males, are bursting with erotic yearnings.

I know we're talking about forty years ago, so to you it may seem like the Dark Ages. But how far we've come as a society and as a church since then is staggering. We might not want to admit that maybe things were better before the sexual revolution even in the church, but we have to ask ourselves: Were infidelity, divorce, and scandal as rampant then?

No, I'm not blaming it all on a new openness to touching and hugging, but I know of people who fell in love because they enjoyed and looked forward to what began as a spiritual expression of brotherly and sisterly love.

I saw this totally from my own narrow, adolescent viewpoint back then. I told myself women weren't as interested in sex as men were, and that adults certainly weren't as sexually on fire as teens. I was way too young to know the difference between the sexual responses of males and females.

I could be turned on by the very *thought* of something sensual. Seeing was even better. Touching, embracing—well, that was just short of making love, wasn't it? What I didn't know then, and what statistics, studies, and experts have proven repeatedly since, is that women are not turned on sexually in the same way men are. They are less likely to be aroused by thought or even sight. They are aroused more slowly, more subtly, but touch plays a major role.

How could I have known then that embracing a woman who belonged to someone else might be almost the culmination of lust on my part, while it might be the beginning of arousal for her? Am I saying that this new freedom to express ourselves to each other is wrong, sinful, dirty, inappropriate? No.

I admit that the church needed some thawing, some warming to each other. Men and women particularly needed to loosen up around each other, talk more, get to know each other better, and, yes, maybe even touch each other once in a while.

Back then, except for the healthy exception of certain ethnic groups, men did not touch each other either—except for a formal or macho handshake, back slap, or thump on the rump during a ball game. I can't speak to the effect this new unpretentiousness might have had on men tormented by a bent toward homosexuality, but one such friend of mine admitted it brought terrible temptation.

As I've grown older, I've acknowledged more of the good that came from the new style. I'm much more comfortable around women, and because it is now appropriate to greet them with a squeeze on the arm or even a warm but proper embrace, I feel better about my relationships. There can be a certain friendly and even spiritual intimacy that doesn't cross the line to impropriety or sensuality. Part of that is due to my own maturity (praise the Lord, the heavy testosterone season of youth is pretty much past), but it is also because of the hedge I'm discussing here.

If I embrace only dear friends or relatives and only in the presence of others, I am not even tempted to make the embrace longer or more impassioned than is appropriate. I like hugging women. It's fun, and it can be friendly. But if I allowed myself to embrace just anyone, even dear friends, in private, I would be less confident of my motives and my subsequent actions.

For instance, what would happen if I just lingered an instant to see what kind of reaction I might get? And let's say that reaction was encouraging. We might both pretend it didn't happen, but what about next time? Would we not be carefully checking each other out to see if what we thought we felt the first time was accurate? And what if it was? At what point would we overtly embrace passionately, silently declaring our feelings for each other?

I don't know, and I don't want to know. That's why I keep such activity public, ensuring its appropriateness.

A FUNNY MEMORY

I have a cousin who's a few years younger than I. She's married and has kids. We've been long-distance buddies for years. Once I was in her state at a writers' conference, and she and her husband invited me for dinner. I waited for her while chatting with a woman from the conference, having idly said my cousin was coming to pick me up.

Oddly, we happened to be discussing this very subject of planting hedges around marriages. The woman had read my magazine article on the subject and was telling me some of the hedges she and her husband had planted.

A car slowly pulled up, and I recognized my cousin behind the wheel. I said my good-byes, but as I hurried out, my cousin left the car and headed toward me. Youthful, tanned, and in shorts, she was striking and attractive. "Your cousin, huh?" the woman said, laughing. "I'll bet!"

My cousin had a child sleeping in a baby seat in the back, and I was tempted to drag him out and display him to prove we had a chaperone. My cousin was normally a person I would embrace after not having seen her for a long time, but

I decided against it for the sake of appearances. She got a good laugh out of the incident.

A NOT-SO-FUNNY MEMORY

Early in my journalism career a young friend of mine went through a trauma with his brother, a wild kind of a guy. The brother lived in Oregon, and though he'd had both a drug and alcohol problem in the past, he somehow landed a job as a security guard. One night after work, while at a party, he scuffled with someone, drew his gun, and shot the man, killing him.

My friend, as you can imagine, was distraught. He worried constantly about his brother. Would he be sentenced? Would he commit suicide? Would he get the death penalty? My friend could hardly work, though his job as a copy boy on the midnight shift was important to our paper.

He was a good friend of the managing editor, a man twenty years his senior. The editor and his wife had taken a liking to the young man and encouraged him in his career. Both had been very sympathetic to his worries over his brother and even helped him financially so he could travel to visit him.

Upon returning from that visit, my friend was convinced his brother was in worse shape emotionally and psychologically than ever. Rather than help calm his fears, the trip had only upset my friend more. He visited the managing editor's home one night, looking for consolation and advice. The editor was gone. The editor's wife embraced my friend and rocked him as he wept for almost half an hour.

This went on for two more nights before my friend came back with the shocking story that this woman, almost a mother figure to him, had made what he considered a pass at him. We scoffed, assuming he was bragging at best, lying at worst. The next night he said he had made out with her for twenty minutes.

She was a woman with a husband who had other priorities. She was a woman who, upon marrying (as Helen Rowland was quoted in *Reader's Digest* years ago), "exchange[d] the attention of all other men she knew for the inattention of one."[1] She was starved for passion, and she found it where she could.

My friend was not without fault, but he was weak and vulnerable. Once she had taken advantage of him, there was no turning back. A marriage ended, and an affair began. There was no future in it for either of them, but they still played it out.

It all started as an innocent, sympathetic embrace, an act of compassion that turned to passion.

DIFFERENT STROKES

This entire subject of hugging and touching may present no problem for you as it does for others. If you have never been turned on by the embrace of a friend, you may think this ridiculous. For you, perhaps it is. But if a person you embrace or who embraces you has a problem, beware.

There are times, places, and situations where physical touch is the only appropriate response. It's therapeutic, loving, and kind. There are other instances where the same response is overkill.

A dear friend of ours recently suffered a terrible tragedy, losing the two people closest to her in the world in an accident in which she also was severely injured. This friend is close enough that I feel free to embrace her in public regularly. Now that she was in the deepest physical and emotional agony a person could endure, I didn't think twice about holding her hand as we talked or even resting my hand on her head as I would with a child in pain. My wife was also there, and this seemed the most logical and normal behavior.

In another context, at another time, a different set of actions would be appropriate. I love this woman in the purest nonromantic sense. I felt deeply for her and wanted her to know it. In another situation or circumstance I would want to guard appearances by responding differently.

The matter of touching and being touched, embracing and being embraced, is as much a matter of common sense and decency as it is of ethnic background and custom. Because of the way I was raised, I tread carefully in this area. If it doesn't happen to be an issue with you, I recommend only that you be sensitive to the attitudes and interpretations of those you choose to touch.

NOTES

1. The *Reader's Digest Treasury of Modern Quotations* (New York: Reader's Digest, 1975), 82.

9

SOME COMPLIMENTS DON'T PAY

Hedge No. 3—If I pay a compliment, it is on clothes or hair-style, not on the person herself. Commenting on a pretty outfit is much different, in my opinion, than telling a woman that she herself looks pretty.

Am I dealing here with only semantics? I think not. I still remember the first time, in the eighth grade, I mustered the courage to tell a girl, "You look nice today." I was so nervous, and gushing that compliment was so disabling, that I never thought to study her reaction.

She thanked me, but clearly I had made her feel uncomfortable too. Was she as affected as I was? I mean, I was a person so afraid of girls at that point that even adding, "How are ya?" at the end of a greeting was too much to consider.

Girls might call me by name and say hi. I would say, "Hi." They would add, "How are ya?" I'd say, "Fine," and keep moving. Why didn't I add, "How are you?"

Conversation, my mother always told me, was like a tennis match. "Someone lobs one to you; you lob it back."

But I was in high school before I marshaled the courage to do that. The results were amazing. A girl I thought was gorgeous greeted me and asked how I was. I said, "Fine" and asked her how she was. She assured me she was great and that she was glad I was fine. And she smiled at me. That alone was enough of a payoff. I had a limited enough self-image to know there was no future in a relationship with her. After all, I hardly knew her, but having a normal, polite, albeit empty conversation with her provided its own euphoria.

So you can see what an accomplishment it had been in junior high to have summoned the fortitude to actually tell a girl she looked nice. I lived on that high for days, realizing only after a week or so that the girl was carefully avoiding me. Had I upset her? Scared her? Made her think I was interested in her? Nothing was worse at that age than having someone after you in whom you were not interested. I wasn't cool or in, wasn't a great dresser, and didn't have money. I was invisible. The only girls I attracted were those who knew they couldn't land someone impressive. When they chased me, I ran. And now I knew how they felt.

I even sent that girl a valentine card, one my brother had dreamed up. It included several small slips of paper with various flowers drawn on them. The card itself was a poem, instructing the recipient to send back to me one of the flowers as a message. For instance, "If I am the one you chose, send me back the big, red rose." There were flowers that would tell me to be patient, to wait, to keep trying, and there was even a dandelion with the verse, "If I waste my time in tryin', send me back the dandelion."

I waited and waited for some response. I was being

ignored and even avoided at school, and it got to the point where I would have been happy even to get the dandelion back. I merely wanted to know if she was aware of my existence. Maybe she had never received the card. The worst possible reaction was no reaction, and that's what I got. Valerie, if you're out there, I need to tell you I'm happily married, and it's too late. If the rose merely got lost in the mail and you thought I had ignored you after that, what can I say except I'm sorry. (I wish I could remember her last name. She sure looked nice that day.)

LESSONS

In retrospect, I realize what I did wrong. Had Valerie been pining away for me, perhaps my compliment on how nice she looked would have thrilled her. But since my approach was clearly a surprise, I should have emphasized the clothes and not the person. I should have been just slightly less personal, which is what I need to do now. I don't have the right to tell a woman how she herself looks, though it might be appropriate to comment on her clothes or hair.

I base part of this hedge on my own reaction to how men talk to my wife. Dianna is tall, dark, and stunning—a head turner. It makes me proud to see men do a double take when they see her. If they keep staring, though, I stare right back until they notice that she's with me.

Dianna is typical of beautiful women who are unaware of their beauty and its impact. If I thought she was looking for compliments it might bother me, but I'm used to the fact that she gets many. And I know she is truly beautiful as opposed to merely sexy, because she gets just as many compliments from women as from men. (In my experience, women compliment each other only on their beauty, not on their seductiveness.)

For some reason, it doesn't bother me if a man comments on my wife's hair or makeup or clothes. But if he should say that she looks pretty or is gorgeous or beautiful, that is too personal. Interestingly, either kind of compliment makes her uncomfortable, but she agrees that the personal approach is worse.

As a hedge, I stop short of the purely personal compliment, because you can never be sure of the reaction. Some women would be offended at such familiarity, and men who talk to women that way tend to get reputations for it. I know a man who is known not only for talking to and about women that way, but also for hanging around them whenever he gets the chance. He always chats with the best-looking women at work, at church, or at a party. At conventions, he spends most of his time at the swimming pool, talking to the best-looking women. I don't know him well enough to know whether his marriage is strong, but you can imagine what people will think if a rumor of infidelity ever makes the rounds. Innocent or not, he won't have a chance to survive it.

I don't get complimented about my looks, but occasionally I'll wear something people like, and they say so. If a woman tells me she likes my tie, jacket, hat, or even my beard, I don't wonder if she's on the prowl or frustrated by a bad marriage. I merely feel complimented.

HEARING VOICES

On the rare occasion when a woman compliments me on the way I look, I confess I'm uncomfortable. Like anyone else, I have certain needs, and among those are what Dr.

James Dobson calls emotional requirements: love, accept-
ance, belonging, caring, and tenderness. My goal is to seek
the fulfillment of those needs within the context of my own
marriage.

Dr. Dobson says there are certain voices that can lure you
from a life of giving yourself to your spouse and children,
working, paying the bills—toward infidelity. These are pleasure ("Come on, have fun; life is passing you by!"), romanticism (someone who cares, someone interested in you as a
person, someone who wants to love you), sex (the pure pleasure of the physical act), and ego needs (someone finds you
attractive for your mind, taste, or talent).

Dr. Dobson ranks sex at the low end of the scale of these
reasons and puts ego needs at the top for both men and
women. For women, he says, romanticism may be a close
second, depending on the health of the marriage, and sex
may be more important to men than to women because of
the differences in biological makeup. The late James L.
Johnson, on the flyleaf of his book *What Every Woman
Should Know About a Man*, called sex "the strange and mys-
terious drive of the God-given chemistry that has shaped
nations, destroyed kingdoms, and brought ruin or ecstasy to
millions from the beginning of time."[1]

The problem with these voices that would lure us from
normal life is that they are lying voices. They promise something other than simply another normal life. But if we run off
with another spouse—even if we do find more pleasure, more
romance, more sex, and more of our ego needs fulfilled—there
is still normal life that has to be dealt with. In fact, it may be
more burdensome than the one we left because of alimony and
child-care expenses from the previous marriage. As Dr.

Dobson says, "The grass may be greener on the other side of the fence, but it still has to be mowed."

GO AHEAD, MAKE HER DAY

The problem with ego needs and the need for romance, especially in a woman's life, is that they are hidden, unseen factors men need to take into consideration when talking to women. We may innocently think it'll make a woman's day if we pay her a compliment that borders on the personal. So, rather than telling her that her sweater is beautiful and asking if she made it (implying that if she made it she's incredible and if she bought it she has great taste), we tell her she looks great in it.

How do we know that perhaps the pleasure and romance and even the sex and ego strokes haven't long since evaporated from her marriage? How do we know that she hasn't been longing for just this sort of attention from her husband? How do we know she hasn't given up on ever getting any more positive strokes from him, and that this very personal approach from us may reach deep needs of which she is hardly aware?

I want to be careful not to make women in bad marriages sound so weak and dependent that they live and die for any personal interest on the part of other men. But in individual cases, we don't know, do we? It never ceases to amaze me when I hear about the latest wife-abuse victim or wife who has been cheated on.

Several years ago a visiting preacher friend counseled the middle-aged wife of a pillar in our church. Her husband, a leading evangelical, had been in the ministry more than forty years.

The story she told the evangelist was incredible. She had been a psychological prisoner in her own home for decades and had been physically abused every few weeks during her entire marriage. She was nearly suicidal, but she had heard something in the evangelist's sermon that gave her a glimmer of hope. My friend told her there was nothing he could do for her until she was prepared to tell someone in authority— her pastor, her husband's superiors, or the police—about her husband. She was unwilling to do that.

Her husband is dead now, and I have lost track of her. Sadly, however, her daughter must have suffered all those years too. A few years after seemingly marrying happily and starting a family—and several years before her father died— she disappeared for a few days and committed suicide a hundred miles from home.

The American College of Obstetricians and Gynecologists reports that three to four million women are beaten in their homes every year.[2]

I share that sordid story to make the point that we never know what kinds of wounds and pains a person carries to church every Sunday. The woman in the account above would probably not have been vulnerable to an approach by any man except for an extremely kind, gentle, godly person. But what about the others? What about those we know just as little about?

No doubt a case could be made for the fact that some women wouldn't know the difference between a compliment of their hair or dress and of themselves as persons. However, there is a difference, even if it registers only subliminally. Planting a hedge that allows you to compliment only a woman's taste in styles and clothes frees you to be friendly, outgoing, and encouraging to women without being suspected of anything worse.

BEST FRIENDS

Years ago I had a boss who told me a story that illustrates the dangers I've been discussing. A friend of his was suspected of taking too much interest in a female teacher at the school where he coached. Bill insisted there was nothing going on, but as rumor after rumor persisted, my friend felt obligated to confront him.

"If there's nothing going on between you and Maggie," my friend said, "why don't you quit spending so much time with her?"

"I like her," Bill said. "And she likes me. Is there anything wrong with having a friend of the opposite sex?"

"It depends on how your wife feels about it," my boss said.

"She hates it, but she's never been a friend to me."

My boss counseled him to break off the relationship. Within six months Bill and Maggie divorced their spouses and married each other. Bill finally confessed to my boss that they had been intimate almost from the beginning. "It all started with my telling her how pretty she looked every day," he said. "She said she had been starved for that kind of attention, because she worked so hard at looking good and no one, she emphasized no one, ever seemed to notice."

"Except you," my boss said.

"Except me," Bill said smiling. He was thrilled. He had found the girl of his dreams. No matter that two marriages and five children had been caught in the typhoon. And neither Bill nor Maggie pledged they would be truer to each other than to their first spouses. Bill never said he would quit complimenting women personally, and Maggie never said she would quit looking for the same from men other than her husband. For Bill to have kept the second marriage intact, he would have had to realize he was competing with anyone who thought his wife looked good and had the guts to tell her.

Apparently he couldn't keep up with the competition. The marriage lasted fewer than four years, and it was she who left him for an older man. (How long would you give that relationship?)

Something about being dumped brought Bill to his senses. He realized what he had done to his wife, and he seemed remorseful. He pleaded with her to take him back. Even though she felt that as a divorced woman she was not free to marry anyone else, she didn't trust him. She was still in such pain that she asked for time to think it over.

He couldn't wait, and he married again. Chaos.

THERE IS A WAY

Sometimes it feels great to compliment a woman other than your wife in a personal way, and you sense it would be a good thing to do. In cases like that, I talk it over with Dianna first. We had a friend who was dumped by her husband, and he tried to justify taking up with another married woman by telling anyone who would listen that despite her image his wife was a shrew—cold, mean, unattractive, and dull.

Maybe behind closed doors she was all that, but my wife and I felt we knew her well enough and had seen her in enough situations to know that she was sweet, spiritual, a good mother, and a loyal and loving wife. She may not have been the hottest thing in town or the most fashionable, but she had certainly done nothing to justify her husband's adultery.

After planning and almost scripting our approach, Dianna and I made sure we ran into her after church one Sunday night. With my arm around my own wife but looking directly into that suffering woman's eyes, I said, "You're not going to let what Benny says convince you that you're not pretty or attractive or exciting, are you?"

She blushed and shook her head. I would not have felt free to say that without my wife at my side. Dianna added, "We know how much you have to offer, and if Benny can't see that, he's just wrong. If he follows through with this, it'll be his loss, not yours."

As a rule we make it a point not to take sides in separations and divorces, but when there is flagrant adultery, we feel little loyalty to the offending party, friend or not.

To quote James Dobson once more, "Marriage is an institution designed to meet individual needs."[3] The key is for husband and wife to meet each other's needs and for other people to mind their own business.

NOTES

1. James L. Johnson, *What Every Woman Should Know About a Man* (Grand Rapids, MI: Zondervan, 1977).

2. "The Silent Epidemic," *Today's Christian Woman*, September/October 2004. Citing statistics from the American College of Obstetricians and Gynecologists. http://www.christianitytoday.com/tcw/2004/005/11.68.html

3. James Dobson, "The Lure of Infidelity," audiocassette from Focus on the Family (1978).

10

LOOKING DOWN THE BARREL OF A LOADED GUN

Hedge No. 4—I avoid flirtation or suggestive conversation, even in jest.

My late father, a police chief, firearms expert, and marksman, once told me that prayer is like looking down the barrel of a loaded gun. "You're likely to get what you're asking for."

I put flirtation and suggestive conversation in the same category as a loaded gun. Maybe that's because I believe in the power of words, written and spoken. Have you ever noticed that compliments and flattery are always heard? People have reminded me of compliments I have given years before and almost forgotten. They remember criticism too, but flattery all the more.

Idle flirting gets people in trouble because the other person needs and wants attention so badly. Not many years ago I slipped from behind this hedge, not intending to flirt but rather to be funny. It didn't get me in serious trouble, but I was certainly reminded of the reason for my hedge.

On a business trip a woman colleague and I were going to go out to dinner with a male associate of ours. When she came to pick me up, she was dressed and made up in flashy, coordinated colors that demanded comment. I should have just said something about her clothes, but instead—since she is always a good audience for my humor—I said the first funny thing that popped into my mind: "My, don't you look delicious."

She laughed, and I hoped she knew I meant that her colors reminded me of fruit, and not that I wished to devour her. As soon as our third party arrived, she told him what I had said. He gave me a look that would have put a wart on a gravestone, but what could I say? I couldn't deny it, and it was too late to explain.

Men, of course, are just as susceptible to flattery as women. Most people think that the man in Proverbs heading down the road of destruction to the harlot's bed had followed his lust for sex. Surely that was part of it, but the text indicates that he also was seduced by her words. Proverbs 7:4-5 says, "Say to wisdom, 'You are my sister' and call understanding your nearest kin, that they may keep you from the immoral woman, from the seductress who flatters with her words." And Proverbs 7:10, 21 says, "There a woman met him, with the attire of a harlot, and a crafty heart. . . . With her enticing speech she caused him to yield, with her flattering lips she seduced him."

KEEP HUMOR IN ITS PLACE

Everyone knows that funny people speak the truth through humor. They may exaggerate how upset they are that someone is late by looking at their watch and saying, "Oh, glad you could make it!" But beneath the joke is a barb of truth. The jokester has slipped in a little lecture without having had to embarrass anyone by saying, "Hey, pal, we agreed on 6 o'clock, and now here you come at 6:30! What's the deal? Get your act together!"

But the same thing happens when someone tries to be funny in a flirtatious manner. A man tells a woman, "Why don't we run off together? Tell that good-for-nothing husband of yours you got a better offer, huh?"

How's a woman supposed to react to that? The first time she may think it's funny because it's so far out of the realm of possibility. Each succeeding time Mr. Comedian says something like that, it gets more irritating. That is, unless the woman has always been attracted to him and has problems at home. Then she might hope there's truth behind the humor.

Often there is. The only time a funny flirter is totally putting someone on is when he throws his arm around a particularly old or homely woman and tries to give her a thrill by saying something she's probably never heard before. "Hey, gorgeous! Where have you been all my life?"

Women like that know better than to believe such drivel, but they may long to hear it anyway. A colleague of mine once toyed with just such a woman by caressing her cheek. "I'm melting," she said, and I sensed she meant it.

The real danger comes when the man is pretending to be teasing, but he'd really love to flirt. A woman may not suspect the truth behind his humor, and if she responds in kind, there is the opportunity for misunderstanding. Or worse, she may indeed suspect that he means it, and then there is the opportunity for real understanding.

Such a tragedy occurred at a church in Michigan where a

couple flirted humorously for almost ten years. They did this in front of everybody, including their spouses, who laughed right along with them. The flirters were never seen alone together, because they never were alone together.

Then came the day when the woman's husband was sick and in the hospital. She needed rides back and forth, and her friend and his wife provided them. No one suspected anything, but on one of those rare occasions when it was just the man doing the driving, the wife of the sick man told him how difficult and cold her husband had been for years.

The flirters began to see each other on the sly until the day came when she told him she had always hoped he'd meant what he said when he had teased her about how wonderful she was, how good she looked, and how he wished he'd met her before she was married. Whether he really meant it was irrelevant now that she had declared herself. The fact was, he admitted later, that this was what he had wanted all along. He would never have made the first move, however. He had hidden his true desires behind a cloak of humor. A little crisis, a little honesty, and suddenly years of innocent flirting had blossomed into an affair.

INNOCENT HUMOR

I worked at a camp one summer during high school. One week one of the women counselors, about a year older than I, shared my last name. We were not related and had never seen each other before. When we were introduced, we had not even made much of the name. While Jenkins is not as common as Smith or Jones, neither is it as unique as Higginbottham or Szczepanik.

One night after the campers were in bed a bunch of us

staffers, Miss Jenkins included, were watching a football game on television. A couple of the guys started kidding her and me about being married. We were both so young and naive and insecure that we just blushed.

For some reason I had to leave before the game was over, and as I headed for the door someone said, "Hey, Jenkins, aren't you takin' your wife with you?"

To prove I could be just as funny as they, I turned and pointed at her. "No, but I want you home in bed in fifteen minutes."

I was out the door when I heard the hooting and hollering. I had not intended even to imply anything risqué. I had merely been trying to go along with the joke, and I meant to speak to her as father to daughter, not husband to wife. Of course, everyone took my wanting her home in bed the wrong way, and I knew I would never live it down. In fact, if I tried to go back and explain, no one would even believe me.

The girl was sweet and chaste, and the last thing I wanted her to think was that I had been inappropriate and had gotten a laugh at her expense. A hundred feet from the cabin, still hearing the laughter, I knew I had to go back.

When I opened the door, no one even noticed me. Something had happened on the game that had everyone's attention. I was glad to see that Miss Jenkins wasn't sitting there weeping with her head in her hands. When I called her name and she looked up, so did everyone else, and the snickering began again.

"Could I see you for a minute?" I said, and the room fell silent.

I'll never forget her response. "I'm not too sure," she said. It was the funniest comeback I could imagine, and I wish I'd anticipated it. Even if my original line had been intentional, hers was better.

The place erupted again. I was grateful when she bounced to her feet and followed me out into the darkness. I had the impression she knew what I was going to say.

"You need to know that I didn't mean that the way it sounded," I said.

"I know," she said.

"You do?"

"Uh-huh."

"I don't think anyone else understands that."

"Maybe not, but I do. I've seen you around, heard you be funny. That's not your style."

"Your comeback was priceless," I said.

"I couldn't pass it up."

"I'm sorry," I said. "I didn't mean to embarrass you."

"Accepted," she said. "And I'm sorry too, though I did mean to embarrass you."

I laughed, and she added, "We Jenkinses have to stick together, you know."

I learned to be more careful about teasing in a flirting manner. I also learned how wonderful and forgiving and insightful some women can be. Funny too.

BY THE SAME TOKEN

Along these same lines, I have made it a practice not to make my wife the butt of jokes. There are enough things to make fun of and enough funny topics without going for easy laughs at the expense of your spouse.

One of the reasons for this is that I would never want Dianna to think I was trying to tell her something serious under the guise of humor. We have made it a policy to speak honestly and forthrightly with each other about anything that bothers us.

We give the lie to the charge that married couples who never fight are probably as miserable and phony as those who fight all the time. We love each other. We don't always agree, and we get on each other's nerves occasionally, but neither of us likes tension in the air. We compete to see who can apologize first and get things talked out. We follow the biblical injunction to never let the sun go down upon our wrath (Ephesians 4:26).

When a group of adult Christians decides it would be healthy to be honest and to share some of their most embarrassing or petty fights, we always confess that we'll either have to pass or make one up. Slammed doors, cold shoulders, silent treatments, and walking out just are not part of our routine. This comes as a result of being careful with our tongues.

Just as I don't want to make the mistake of flirting in jest or being suggestive in conversation with anyone but my wife, I want to watch what I say to her too. Scripture has a lot to say about the power of the tongue and the spoken word. Proverbs 18:21 says that death and life "are in the power of the tongue," and Proverbs 21:23 says, "Whoever guards his mouth and tongue keeps his soul from troubles."

Proverbs 28:23 says, "He who rebukes a man will find more favor afterward than he who flatters with the tongue." In the New Testament, James says that the tongue is a little member but that it boasts great things. "See how great a forest a little fire kindles!" (James 3:5).

Flattery, flirtation, suggestive jesting, and what we say to our own spouses are all shades of the same color. Beware the power of the tongue.

II

MEMORIES

Hedge No. 5—I remind my wife often—in writing and orally—that I remember my wedding vows: "Keeping you only unto me for as long as we both shall live." Dianna is not the jealous type, nor has she ever demanded such assurances. She does, however, appreciate my rules and my observance of them.

People seem to take their wedding vows so cavalierly nowadays that you have to wonder if they have any idea what they're saying. Census figures show that one of every four marriages performed in 1931-33 ended in divorce. By the mid-fifties the rate had jumped to one in three. A few years later it hit 41 percent.[1]

According to *The Barna Update* of September 2004, among all adults who have been married, 35 percent have also been divorced, and 3 percent are presently separated. Eighteen percent of adults who have ever been divorced have been divorced more than once.[2]

While, according to The National Marriage Project's "The State of Our Unions," divorce has declined slightly since the early 1980s, "for the average couple marrying in recent years, the lifetime probability of divorce or separation remains close to 50 percent."[3]

It may be naive to think that people would remain true to their vows just by repeating them frequently, but who knows? At least couples might come to really understand what they said in a ceremony before God, friends, and spouse.

PRACTICAL SUGGESTIONS

There are many creative ways to remind your spouse and yourself of your wedding vows, and they can be adapted to any budget. Try surprising your wife with a progressive search that culminates in a trip somewhere special. If you can afford it, take her out of the country. If you can't, drive to the next town for a weekend at a hotel. Or even just to McDonald's.

Set it up this way:

Write out slips that contain your wedding vows, particularly those that refer to remaining sexually faithful, in a rhyme or even a short-story format. At the end of each slip, leave a clue that leads to where your wife can find the next one. Then hide them around the house and in the garage.

Mail the first one home. It might say, "Keeping you—" and then "Look for another message in the freezer."

When she looks in the freezer, she finds another slip that reads, "—only unto me—" and "Look for another message in the car."

In the car is a slip that reads, "—for as long—" and points her to the mantel over the fireplace. There she finds a note that says, "—as we both—" and "Look for another message in the junk drawer." There she will find a message that reads, "—shall live." There you might also plant a plane ticket or hotel reservation or baby-sitting certificate or McDonald's gift certificate.

It can be just as effective, though maybe not as much fun, simply to call her at home or at work, and tell her, "I made this vow _____ years/months/days ago, and I still mean it: 'I will keep you only unto myself for as long as we both shall live, or until Christ, who has saved us by His grace, returns to take us unto Himself forever.'"

Sending your vows in a telegram or mailgram can be effective. E-mail is a little too easy and cheap, but it's better than nothing. You might even have someone pen your vows in calligraphy or have it printed so you can decoupage it. I've heard of people having their vows written in icing on a cake, chiseled into a rock, burned into wood, even written in moist dirt in the front yard. A friend of mine spent a couple of hours forming the letters to his vows in tiny bits of twig, then set them up on the cement slab in front of the door of his house, only to see his wife miss their significance and sweep them off the porch onto the grass.

Sometimes I like to just tell Dianna that I remember my vows and that she is the only woman I have ever slept with, and the only one I ever wish to sleep with. I usually add my own sentiments on anniversary, valentine, and birthday cards too. I don't think she ever tires of hearing me reiterate my vows. I know I never get tired of hearing or saying them.

WHAT'S GOOD FOR THE GOOSE

The sad fact is that there is simply not enough emphasis on wedding vows anymore. We need to face it: This is one of the most significant problems in modern marriage. I've never understood the long-standing double standard that seems to wink at males' infidelity while holding women in contempt for the same offense. Of course, the breaking of a sacred vow should not be tolerated for either sex, but there is a boys-will-be-boys mentality that allows some men—even Christians—to have occasional or long-standing mistresses their entire married lives.

As we've seen countless marriages break up during our thirty-plus years together, Dianna and I have talked seriously about this issue. Divorce is not in our vocabulary, but we have discussed whether either of us could forgive the other for the ultimate in unfaithfulness and betrayal.

Early in our marriage Dianna told me she didn't think she was capable of forgiving sexual unfaithfulness. Though I had, of course, never considered violating my vows, it was impressive to hear that. I tried to imagine the shoe on the other foot and decided the same. The thought of sleeping with my wife after she had been unfaithful was inconceivable. It still is, but both of our views have grown on this subject.

We have seen friends' and relatives' marriages shattered by adultery, and yet we have also counseled spouses to forgive each other and take each other back. Regaining trust after adultery still seems impossible, and neither of us has come to the point where we will say unequivocally that we could take back the other after unfaithfulness. We admit, though, that there are other things to consider.

For instance, we have seen that adultery is usually not the major problem in bad marriages. It is more often the result of a bad marriage or the symptom of a bad marriage. It may be the worst thing that can happen to a marriage, but it is rarely the basic problem. We hope and trust and believe and pray that any of our discussions about this subject are academic in our own marriage because we work so hard at it, but adultery does occasionally invade even seemingly solid marriages.

Take the case of a Christian leader who stepped down from an executive position with a mission organization ten years ago after his adultery was revealed. His wife, his pastor, and a couple of close relatives already knew of his sin and also of his repentance. When it came to light, however, he realized that resigning was the only way to protect the reputation of the mission and keep it from extended controversy.

Anyone who knew this man knew he had been a model husband and father. Even his wife and children said so. Thus the shocking moral lapse was clearly not the result of a pattern in his life or of a bad marriage. He admitted that during a period of burnout and extreme fatigue, he allowed a friendship to become immoral, and he apparently sincerely repented.

Most interesting was that his wife not only forgave him but has also said that she would not dwell on his short period of unfaithfulness. To their credit, neither discounted that he had sinned, that his actions were unacceptable, or that he needed to repent and ask for forgiveness from God and all affected individuals. Some feel he has forever disqualified himself from the ministry, but my purpose here is to deal with the forgiveness aspect.

If he was truly repentant, did his wife have a choice as a Christian to do anything but forgive him and welcome him back? Whereas many believe that adultery is biblical grounds for divorce, surely divorce is not mandated when the offending party is remorseful and wants to reconcile.

Therefore, even though both Dianna and I cannot imagine

finding within ourselves the wherewithal to forgive the other should adultery ever disgrace and defile our marriage, clearly the biblical, Christian response to a repentant sinner is forgiveness. In ourselves, in our flesh, this would probably not be possible. Only through Christ can divine, unconditional love find forgiveness for a spouse who has foisted the filthiest pollution on a marriage.

Even as Dianna and I continue to struggle with the proper response—and continue also to pray against such a problem and work toward a marriage that will not allow it—we counsel those who have been victimized to forgive the offending spouse if he or she is willing to reconcile. We can only pray that we could be as charitable to each other, as unthinkable as that is to us now.

One thing is certain. Marriages in which the ultimate loss of trust has been suffered can never be the same. We can only imagine what a wife who has taken back a husband who slept with another woman, or vice versa, must go through when that offending spouse wants to enjoy the marriage bed again. How long would it be—if ever—before either could forget that the vows had been broken, that one of them had not kept the other only unto himself or herself? Could deep, abiding trust ever be fully regained? No wonder few marriages survive such an onslaught.

Although I would probably want more than anything to reconcile with my wife after such a failure, I certainly wouldn't be able to blame her if she simply was not able to forgive that outrageous transgression of her trust. And though if I were the offended party I cannot fathom being able to put her sin out of my mind, I'd like to think I would not turn away my truly repentant wife whom I love.

Even considering that jumble of horrifying emotions is so distasteful that all it does is make me want to emphasize again the whole reason for this book. Again I need to say that adultery is usually a result or symptom of a marriage with weaknesses throughout. If protecting your marriage requires occasionally running through your mind's eye being caught or having to confess to your wife that you have been unfaithful, then I recommend that exercise.

You won't find it pleasant. Imagine breaking down as you tell her, hoping she'll understand, seeing her turn away cold and hurt, not wanting to be touched or to hear any more. My guess is that the typical woman won't want to see her husband's tears of grief and remorse right away. He will tumble off whatever pedestal he may have been on, and should she ever find it within herself, by the grace of God, to forgive him and take him back, it will not be without deep pain and suffering.

Imagine, just imagine, what that would do to *your* wife. Plant hedges wide and deep and tall against any weakness you may have. Remind yourself what price you would have to pay for a brief season of carnal fun. Study what is wrong within you or in your relationship with your wife that would allow you even to consider such a drastic breach of her trust.

Dianna and I had college friends who were married ten years and had two sons when we first got wind there was trouble. The wife suspected her husband was seeing another woman. We stood by her, helped her find out, confronted him, heard the denials, and then learned the awful truth: It was true.

He was unrepentant, hostile, and flagrant. He had complaints about his wife, but none justified this complete setting aside of his morals and values. She kept fighting for him, wanting him back. We warned her that until he gave up the other woman and—in essence—came back on his knees, she should be slow to open her arms. Maybe we were intruding rather than helping, but she received similar counsel from others.

Still, she was desperate. She couldn't stand the thought of losing him to someone else. No, she was not the woman he had married. She had given birth to both sons within a year of each other, and she had grown weary and harried trying to keep up with them. Maybe she had become shrill, and maybe she had neglected him, but he had never grown up either. Now he played most of the time and was gone more than he was home. And now this—another woman.

She moved in with her aunt and took the boys with her. He begged her to come back, promising to change his ways. It was all she wanted to hear. She set conditions: "Give up the other woman, spend time at home, don't expect Olympic sex after this rupture of my trust, and grow up."

The first night they spent together, he got a call from the other woman. "Take that call and I'm out of here," his wife told him.

"Just some loose ends," he assured her, and they talked on the phone for a half hour. Then he left. "Just getting some stuff, settling accounts. Don't worry. It's over."

He was gone all night and still tried to tell her nothing had happened. But he had pushed his wife past the brink. She packed up the boys and all her belongings and moved out. Even while he was again trying to plead with her to take him back, a friend saw his car in front of his girlfriend's house all night. The friend left a note, berating him for living a lie. That finally brought him to his senses.

From what we could tell, he had finally truly repented. He'd come back to God, cut off the relationship, and done everything he could to win back his wife.

But do you know what? It was too late. If she had been Jesus, she might have forgiven him seventy times seven, and there were those who felt she was being cold and unforgiving and even unchristian. Sadly, he had pushed her too far. I'm not saying she was right, but she got to the place of rage, and suddenly she could believe nothing he said and could trust nothing he promised. She could only suspect everything he did.

The story is twenty years old now, and both partners have been married again. She has divorced for the second time. We're talking about Christian people. Adultery creates chaos. Adulterers lie. Victims get angry. There are human limits to forgiveness, even among Christians.

Somehow, some way we who have remained true to our spouses need to do something to ensure we continue that way. That means working on our weaknesses, shoring up our strengths, pouring our lives into each other, and planting hedges. We must avoid the mess of adultery and divorce and the besmirching of the reputation of Christ. The time is long past for us to worry about people snickering at us for being prudish or Victorian or puritanical.

Treat this blight on marriage as the epidemic it is. Flee. Plant a hedge. Do something. Anything. Don't become a sad statistic.

NOTES

1. *The Reader's Digest Treasury of Modern Quotations* (New York: Reader's Digest, 1975), 83.

2. "Born Again Christians Just As Likely to Divorce as Are Non-Christians" *The Barna Update*, September 8, 2004. http://www.barna.org/FlexPage.aspx?Page=BarnaUpdate&BarnaUpdateID=170

3. *The National Marriage Project*, eds. Barbara Dafoe Whitehead and David Popenoe, "The State of Our Unions," 2004 (Rutgers, NJ: The State University of New Jersey, June 2004). http://marriage.rutgers.edu/Publications/SOOU/SOOU2004.pdf

12

QUALITY TIME VS. QUANTITY TIME

Hedge No. 6—From the time I got home from work until the children went to bed, I did no writing or office work. That gave me lots of time with the family and for my wife and me to continue to court and date.

Something subtle but unusual happened after Dianna and I had been married about a year. I had recently left the field of secular journalism and had begun working for Scripture Press Publications. Among my duties was interviewing people for stories for Sunday school papers.

Coincidentally several of my interviews during a short span were with men about twice the age I was then. Their stories were all different, but eventually we got around to the subjects of home and marriage and family, and I asked each if he had any regrets at this stage of his life. To a man, every one said he wished he'd spent more time with his kids during their growing-up years.

Their marriages had been fine, and their children had turned out okay, but everyone had a lot of "if onlys."

- "If only I'd realized my daughter's recital was more important than the big real estate deal . . ."
- "If only I could have proved to my son how proud I was of him by showing up at his games . . ."
- "If only my wife had known before she died how much I enjoyed talking with her and traveling with her . . ."

It's become a cliché by now that no one has ever been heard to say on his deathbed, "I wish I'd spent more time at the office."

These expressions of regret over misplaced priorities during the sunny years of their careers—which always seem to coincide with the growing-up years of a man's family—had little to do with their stories and didn't wind up in the pages of Scripture Press's Sunday school papers. But I sensed God had put me in contact with these men for a reason: They all sent me the same message. I was barely twenty-two years old, but I caught the drift. If I had those same regrets at their age, I would be without excuse.

I remember a lengthy discussion with Dianna about this. We wouldn't have our first child until we'd been married four and a half years; so that gave us a lot of time to set goals, policies, and priorities. We wanted to be good parents and avoid regrets.

We decided that once the children came along, I would do no writing and no office business between the time I got home from work and the time the kids went to bed. (I've been accused of sometimes putting them to bed at 4:30!)

In the beginning the biggest benefit was Dianna's. She had someone to take over feeding and changing and entertaining a baby while she finally had time to fix dinner. Sometimes baby Dallas was sleeping when I got home, but that didn't count; he had to be down for the night before I felt free to get into my own projects.

When Chad came along two and a half years later, Dallas had already learned to take for granted that I would be around during that time of the day. I didn't insist that the boys honor the time I had carved out for them or even that they interact with me. I just wanted them to get used to the fact that I was theirs to talk to, to play with, or even to ignore.

I learned that the idea of quality time was a lie. Some experts espoused the idea that successful overachievers could be guilt-free about the little time they were able to devote to their children if only they invested quality time when they could. It was sort of like one-minute parenting. Just be sure that what little time you are able to spend with your child is quality time, those experts said.

What garbage. I've seen the results of kids who were given only quality time. The problem is that kids don't know the difference. What they need is time—all they can get. Quantity time *is* quality time, whether you're discussing the meaning of the cosmos or just climbing on Dad.

There were times I wished my kids knew how wonderful I was being about all this. I didn't know many fathers who gave their kids at least two and a half hours a day—and there certainly weren't any other fathers who played ball with the whole neighborhood every summer afternoon.

But of course this was not all just for the kids' benefit. I can't imagine missing their growth experiences or the funny and touching things they said, and even having been there in times of crisis when I could easily have been somewhere else.

There came a point when Dallas, at about age four, told me he wished he had a new dad. "Like who?" I asked him.

"Like the man down the street," he said. I knew exactly who he was talking about and why.

The man down the street came home so infrequently that he got a royal welcome every time he did. And he was usually feeling so guilty about his drinking or topless-barhopping or compulsive spending that he brought gifts for everyone. What a guy! What a dad! He must be super to get that kind of reception and be so generous!

I couldn't explain the distinctions to Dallas until he was old enough to understand why the man down the street left his wife a note one morning, telling her she would find him in the garage with the car running. He had committed suicide.

SO WHAT?

What does all this have to do with marital hedges? Hedges can do wonders for a family, and this policy of spending megablocks of time with the kids each day turned into rich benefits for Dianna and me too. Our time together was more relaxed, less hurried, less pressured, less obligatory. We learned to just be with each other, to be used to having each other around. We don't have to talk, plan, schedule, or make appointments with each other. We know each other's schedules, and we count on when the other will be available. Dianna tells me that she enjoyed a tremendous sense of satisfaction and well-being when I was devoting time to the kids. She never felt left out or jealous, especially since she and I also spent a lot of time together.

Our sons are now all in their twenties. Two are married, and one is a father of three. Dallas, Chad, and Mike soon figured out, of course, that their relationship with their parents was out of the ordinary, at least as it relates to the amount of time spent together. We hardly ever missed one of their church, school, or sports events, and we were never gone from home more than a certain number of days without taking them with us. Our trip to Africa in 1989 was one of the richest family times we ever had.

More important, the kids saw a difference in our marriage too. They knew we were still affectionate and in love and demonstrative about it even after all those years. The boys became eager to know the whys and wherefores of all our ideas and behavior. So I told them about our hedges and why we feel they're so important.

They were intrigued, and I've seen evidence of their doing the same in their relationships. Having my sons know about my hedges really serves as another hedge in itself. Just like my friend who carries pictures of his wife and daughters as a hedge on business trips, I carry the knowledge that my kids are aware of my concern for our marriage. They and our grand-children would be front-line victims if we let down our guard.

Another of our traditions was that until our kids became teenagers, I put them to bed every night I was home. We talked, read, sang, memorized Scripture, and prayed together. Following a tradition set by my own father, I took that oppor-tunity, too, to say nice things about their mother. "Don't we have a great mom? Isn't she good to us? Do you have any idea how much she loves you? Do you know she works at least twice as hard as Dad? Aren't you proud that she always looks so nice?"

A ROSE BY ANY OTHER NAME

I thought of how important the strength of a marriage is to children when I saw a quote by Pete Rose, Jr. The betting scandal his baseball star father got caught in meant little to Petey. He still dwelt on his parents' years-old divorce. His father was remarried with a new child and another on the way. His mother was tending bar in Cincinnati.

Petey was a better-than-average big-league prospect himself, and athletes at that stage in their careers are usually single-minded and driven. Yet Petey said something like this: "I would trade whatever future I have in big league baseball to see my parents get back together."[1]

It was as if he hadn't read the papers and didn't know the truth about his parents' marriage. Pete, Sr. had such a reputation for chasing women and such nasty, impossible-to-take-back things had been said by each about the other that no one would give two cents for the possibility of civility, let alone reconciliation. And with Pete, Sr. remarried, there was no chance. Yet that comment from little Pete, if he were my son, would haunt me to my grave. The fact is, that's a common theme from adult children of divorce.

LOVE ME, LOVE MY MOM

The following statement has been attributed to everybody from Howard Hendricks to Josh McDowell to James Dobson. It probably preceded all three, but it remains true: The most important thing a father can do for his children is to love their mother. When we know that one of the great fears of childhood is abandonment, we can only imagine the impact of a broken marriage on a child.

MAY "THE VORCE" NOT BE WITH YOU

Several years ago *Campus Life* magazine ran a story about "the vorce," which represented a child's misunderstanding of the word *divorce*. A child in the story said that sometimes people even talk about "the the vorce," which she couldn't understand at all. All she knew was that anytime anyone ever talked about "the vorce" or "the the vorce," it was sad and bad news. It had something to do with Mommy and Daddy, and she didn't like the vorce.[2]

It reminded me of a little girl I knew when I was seven. I thought she was the sweetest, cutest four-year-old I had ever seen. Because of our difference in age I didn't see much of her during the next few years, but by the time she was nine she was a sad little creature with a drawn face and red eyes. The only thing she would tell her Sunday school teacher was that she was afraid of the vorce. Her teacher thought she meant some kind of force, but soon the truth came out.

Her parents were leaders in the church and seemed to have an idyllic family with several children, including a couple of adoptees. More than once, however, the children had been awakened in the night to their parents' arguing, even yelling and screaming. That was when this pretty little girl had first heard about the vorce. Her mother was pleading with her father not to get the vorce. Whatever it was, the little girl knew it was bad.

Divorcées will tell you that children are resilient, that a divorce is better for a child than a bad marriage. But experts in child psychology tell a different story. Some kids who bottle up their emotions and pretend it's all right to be shuttled back and forth between parents and cities, often by air, grow up emotional wrecks. They're unable to trust or fully love anyone. They fear rejection, suffer low self-esteem, careen in and out of their own doomed marriages, and leave in their wakes children just like themselves.

Donna Kato, in her article "Children Suffer More from Divorce Than Previously Thought," cites a study coauthored by family expert Judith Wallerstein and San Francisco State University professor Julia Lewis, which looked at 130 children aged two to six from sixty families. They are now between twenty-seven and thirty-two.

"Studying and interviewing the children at intervals that ranged from every 18 months to five years," Wallerstein reached several conclusions, including:

> That divorce affects children psychologically, economically, and socially. Half of the young people in the study, for example, were involved in serious drug and alcohol abuse, many before the age of 14.[3]

Another landmark study found that nine of ten children of divorce suffered a sense of shock at the separation, "including profound grieving and irrational fears."[4] Half reported feelings of rejection and abandonment.[5] And 37 percent were more "unhappy and dissatisfied five years after the divorce than they had been at 18 months."[6]

This is the generation growing up now. What must most family reunions and family trees look like? What kinds of adults will be running our corporations, leading our government, pioneering technological progress?

We can grow paranoid, I guess, but with the skyrocketing divorce rate wreaking havoc on the minds and emotions of that many children, mayhem seems the only prognosis. The only way to ensure a future with stable marriages and home lives is to begin strengthening our families now. Give kids a model of love and caring and interdependence. Show them what it means to make and keep a commitment, to set your course on a lifetime of love with no wavering, no excuses, and no me-first philosophies.

Don't fall prey to the quality time trap or to the myth that kids are resilient and will be better off in two halves of a broken home. Most children of divorce are just like Pete Rose, Jr. They'd give up everything else in their lives if only their parents would get back together. Make a decision. Set a course. Carve out the time it takes to devote yourself to your wife and children, and plant a hedge that will protect you and her and them from the devastation of a broken home.

NOTES

1. Mike Bass, *Cincinnati Post*, as printed in the *Chicago Tribune*, March 28, 1989, 5.
2. M. J. Amft, "The Vorce and Other Questions," *Campus Life*, January 1978, 43.
3. Donna Kato, "Children Suffer More from Divorce Than Previously Thought," *San Jose Mercury News*, June 3, 1997.
4. Judith S. Wallerstein, and Joan B. Kelly, *Surviving the Breakup* (New York: Basic Books, 1980), 33.
5. Ibid., 48.
6. Ibid., 211.

PART THREE

WHAT HEDGES CAN DO FOR YOUR FAMILY

Telling your story, speaking openly of the hedges in your marriage, protecting yourself and your family from insidious new sources of unacceptable media, and truly practicing the Golden Rule at home will give your spouse and your children a deep sense of love and security.

13

EVERYBODY LOVES A LOVE STORY

It's important to share with your spouse and children the memories of your own courtship, marriage, and honeymoon. And it's never too late to recall the memories of your early love. The longer you go without doing it, the easier it is to forget important details. But by telling your story over and over through the years, you solidify in your mind the things that attracted you to your mate in the first place. Just as important, your children learn the history of the relationship.

I was always fascinated by the stories my parents told about how they met, fell in love, and stayed true to each other during their engagement, although World War II kept them apart for thirty-four months before they married in 1945.

There are various ways of reminding one another and your children of your own love story. Obviously it's not a good idea to force the story on casual acquaintances or neighbors—unless they ask—but you'd be surprised at how many people are indeed interested: old friends, close relatives, people from church you know well. Trade stories with them. Everybody loves a love story.

I share my own story here only to show the types of memories you can ferret out to share with your mate. I call it my own, rather than our own, because every courtship is really two stories, yours and your spouse's. Dianna's story contains parallel elements, of course, but the emphases are hers, and her perspective provides an account with its unique interest.

Every time we tell our stories, we remind each other of incidents we hadn't thought of since they occurred in the early 1970s. Every birthday, anniversary, holiday, or no-reason-I-just-felt-like-sending-a-card occasion provides an opportunity for a note or a comment, maybe just a sentence from our wedding vows to share with each other. Repeat a wedding vow in your spouse's ear the next time you kiss hello or good-bye. There's no reason not to in some small way celebrate your wedding anniversary every day. If you have a good marriage, build a hedge around it by celebrating it. Think how unique a gift you have been blessed with in this generation of divorce.

MY STORY

I had not dated for a year when a friend and his fiancée began telling me of a girl I just had to meet, a classmate of theirs at Fort Wayne (Indiana) Bible College. She was tall and beautiful, they told me. Oh, sure, I thought. That's why she has to resort to blind dates.

I got a look at her from afar when I visited the campus and saw her in the homecoming court. They were right. She was gorgeous. So much so that I was intimidated. No way would I have dreamed she had a night free, let alone that she would accept a date with me. I'd waste my time and pride by asking her out.

"But we've told her about you," my friends said. "She's open to a blind date."

"Forget it," I said. "I've seen her. She hasn't seen me."

But my interest was piqued. Maybe someday.

Someday came a few months later. They talked me into driving over from Chicago for a double date. Ever the romantic, I started building the possibilities in my mind. I told myself that if anything was to come from this, I would know immediately and be smitten with her.

The blind date on a Friday night in May 1970 was fine. She was lovely, refined, soft-spoken, smart, likable, and easy to talk to. But there were no whistles, bells, or fireworks. As soon as he got me alone, my friend wanted to know what I thought.

"Fine," I said.

"Just fine?"

I nodded.

"Could you get interested? Try to build something?"

"Nah. I don't know. I don't think so."

"Why? Something wrong?"

"No. We just didn't click."

"You've had one date!"

"Yeah, but I'd know."

"You're crazy."

"Maybe I am."

The next night we doubled again, and my reaction was the same. Dianna and I promised to write, and, feeling polite and benevolent, I said maybe I would visit her again. We corresponded occasionally over the next few weeks, and I sensed

Dianna was more interested than I was. In fact, if she had not gently pressed that I had said I would come back, I probably wouldn't have. (Frankly, that circumstance is not something I dwell on.)

Dianna told me later that at the wedding of the friends who had introduced us, she sensed my lack of enthusiasm. I was busy in the wedding party and only really spoke to her as she was leaving. For some reason, just before she got into her car I touched the tip of her nose and said good-bye. She took it as the only bit of encouragement she had.

Before I finally drove back to see her in Fort Wayne on July 18, I had the audacity to tell my friend that if everything went the same as before, I was not going to pursue the relationship. "You're crazy," he said.

This time it would not be a double date. She was going to cook dinner for us at her place, and then we would walk around The Landing, an old section of Fort Wayne. I pulled in the driveway and went to the front door. As I rang the bell I could see Dianna through the screen door, heading for the kitchen.

"Come on in," she said. "I have to catch something on the stove."

She flashed a smile as she hurried past, and something happened to me. After two double dates and a brief chat at our friends' wedding, it was love at fourth sight. Dianna says the only difference since I had seen her last was her tan. That makes me sound pretty shallow, but there it is. I don't know what clicked. All I know is that it was the most dramatic emotion I have ever felt, before or since.

I hardly knew the woman, but I was struck dumb and

knew beyond doubt that I would marry her. I don't know how I knew, but I knew it as surely as I knew my own name. I followed her into the kitchen, literally unable to say a word. (Anyone who knows me knows how unique that had to be.) If she had asked me how the drive was, I would have been able to manage only a nod.

Dianna is most comfortable when someone else is carrying the conversation. One of the things she liked about me was that I enjoyed talking, drawing people out. And there I stood, like a dolt.

She acted as if she didn't notice and uncharacteristically chattered about the chicken, the vegetables, the salad. I watched her slice carrots, thinking, *She is going to do this in our home someday. I'll watch her do this for the rest of my life.* I can't explain it. I just knew, and I never wavered.

When I finally spoke, my voice cracked, and I noticed her double take. What an ordeal that meal was! Dianna grew up on a farm and was a 4-H champion cook; so the food was wonderful. But I sat trying to make small talk, all the while hiding my delicious secret: I was going to marry this girl. She had seemed more interested in me than I in her, but now I had shot past her by light-years.

Dianna and I were impressed by different little things that night. I was impressed that a basically shy girl felt comfortable enough to put her feet up on a chair during the meal. Later, as we strolled The Landing, holding hands for the first time, she was impressed that I wouldn't let her run to the car when it began to rain. She worried about her naturally curly hair. Nothing could have made her less beautiful to me.

Later we drove to a park in the center of the city where

we walked in the rain. It was one of those nights that nearly every couple has at one time or another. We talked of everything, learned of childhood memories, quizzed each other on favorite colors, foods, tastes in clothes, books—anything that came to mind. I was in paradise.

I could hardly contain my secret. I wanted to tell her something, anything, that would alert her that to me this was much, much more than a typical date or even a new relationship. It made no sense, but I knew to the core of my being that this was it. She would be my wife, and nothing anyone did could change that.

Before I left her for the two-hour drive back to Chicago at midnight, I pretended to be kidding and told her I thought I was already falling in love. She found that funny, and I was glad I hadn't seriously revealed my heart. By the time I got in the car, whether it made sense or not, I was helplessly, wholly in love. I thought I had been in love before, but now I knew better.

All the way to Chicago I sang, whistled, talked to myself, and tried to think of someone I could tell. One of my friends worked in an all-night gas station in my home town. I arrived at 2 in the morning, grinning from the waist up. I went into the station and sat on a fifty-five-gallon oil drum, beginning a three-and-a-half-hour rhapsody.

"I want you to be in our wedding," I concluded.

My friend shook his head. "You've got it bad."

I didn't know how right he was until I climbed down off that oil drum at 5:30 in the morning and realized I'd been sitting in a quarter inch of motor oil the whole time! It had soaked through my seat and down my pant legs, even into my socks. (It felt pretty good, actually.)

With the morning newspaper between me and my car seat, I arrived home at 6 in the morning and peeked into my parents' bedroom. My mother opened one eye.

"You're in love," she said.

She couldn't have paid me a higher compliment. I couldn't get over that it showed, and Mom hadn't even seen the oil yet.

I didn't sleep for a couple of days, but I did start on what would become astronomical phone bills over the next several months. I tried as hard as I could not to let my temporary insanity show through, but I failed. Dianna didn't know what to make of it, and when she visited Chicago one weekend, my secret was out. For the next several months I tried not to make a fool of myself, and she carefully considered this new friend who had started with such ambivalence and was now racing ahead of her own feelings.

During that period I discovered the depth of the woman I was convinced would be my wife. Before long my infatuation matured to true love. By September Dianna shared my feelings, and we began to discuss our future. In November she suggested a brief moratorium on the relationship. We had known each other such a short time and were talking so seriously of marriage that she wanted to back off for a couple of weeks and sort out her feelings.

I was devastated.

I didn't tell Dianna, but I was convinced she was doing this only because it was the type of thing her friends had done. Worse, I dreaded that she would come to her senses and realize she could do so much better. I believed that if I ever heard from her again, it would be in the form of a Dear John letter or a phone call suggesting that we should be just friends.

This was, of course, years before Dr. James Dobson's excellent book *Tough Love*, which advises the waiting party in such a relationship to maintain dignity. Part of me wanted to beg and plead and cry and ask how Dianna could do such a thing to a person willing to crawl in front of her for the rest of her life, licking up dirt so she wouldn't have to step in it. Wouldn't that have been a nice example of the kind of man a woman wants for a husband?

I resisted the urge to grovel, but I did a lot of tearful walking and praying. In retrospect, I was a sniveling weakling who somehow had enough foresight to keep it to himself. But at the time I was in real turmoil. I believed Dianna was meant for me, that only she could make me happy. I held to the conviction that we were meant to be married.

But I had to come to the point with God where I was willing to give her up. I had to get to the place where I conceded that if I truly loved her, then I would want what was best for her. If what was best for Dianna was not me, then that was what I wanted for her. Otherwise, my love was selfish. It was not easy. In fact, it was the most difficult ordeal of my life. But after four days of agony I made that concession. I didn't feel much better, and I did not want things to turn out that way, but I knew I had done the right thing by being willing to accept it.

That night she called.

"Enough of this nonsense," she said. "I miss you. Come when you can."

I drove four hours to see her for half an hour, then drove back home. We were married within three months.

I don't begrudge her the four days she needed. I am glad she didn't need the entire two weeks. I would have been a basket case. Whatever she settled in her mind during those few days has lasted our entire marriage. For whatever grief it caused me then, it has afforded me a wife with no second thoughts.

PEORIA?

Clearly, that story is of real interest only to those involved, including our children. When they were living at home, they often insisted on hearing it. They liked to hear about the wedding, too, giggling over my father pushing the Play button rather than the Record button on his tape recorder at the worst possible moment during the ceremony. While the pastor exhorted us, we were treated to ten seconds of a business seminar Dad was trying to tape over.

We wrote our own vows, borrowing ideas from friends. We promised each other that we would "keep you only unto me," but rather than the morbid "till death do us part," we used the more hopeful "for as long as we both shall live, or until Christ, who has saved us by His grace, returns to take us unto Himself forever."

I also vowed to make Dianna laugh, which I have tried to do daily for more than three decades. (If I've failed by the end of the day, I sometimes resort to swinging from the chandelier.)

We were married in downstate Illinois and left the next day to drive across the country for a job in Washington state. So we spent our first honeymoon night at the Holiday Inn in Peoria. It didn't seem at all funny then, but that gets the biggest smile today when we recount our story.

Tell your story. Tell it to your kids, your friends, your brothers and sisters, but especially to each other. The more your story is implanted in your brain, the more it serves as a hedge against the myriad forces that seek to destroy your marriage. Make your story so familiar that it becomes part of the fabric of your being. It should become a legend shared through the generations as you grow a family tree that defies all odds and boasts marriage after marriage of stability, strength, and longevity.

14

WHEN VICTORY COMES

Something wonderful happens in a relationship when hedges begin to grow. It's crucial to understand that the hedges I've discussed have been my own, tailor-made for an oversexed, gregarious, fun-loving, busy person who might otherwise follow his lusts, say things he shouldn't, flirt, forget the most important person in his life, and not spend as much time with his family as he should.

Your weaknesses may be different. Some might make me laugh or make me think you're a nut, as some of mine may have done to you. The important thing is to know yourself, understand the dangers in your weak areas, and do something practical and concrete about them.

The case studies that follow are of two couples who have learned the hard way to plant their own hedges. Their hedges bear little resemblance to mine. That's the point.

Names and insignificant details have been changed to protect identities.

IKE AND LAURIE VANDERAY

Ike is a successful independent insurance agent in the South. Laurie worked early in their marriage but became pregnant almost immediately, and they now have five children under age eleven. They were a passionate, exciting couple during their long courtship, but financial setbacks, health problems, and two miscarriages made early married life difficult.

Seven pregnancies in a dozen years have not been a problem for Laurie. She loves babies, was heartbroken over the two losses, and is even interested in maybe having one more. Both Vanderays are very active in their local church, serving in Sunday school and in the choir and on various boards and committees. Ike is also very visible in community affairs for the sake of his business.

Ike has found that Saturdays can be big in his line of work. People who can't see him during the work week will often schedule a Saturday appointment. Laurie pleaded with him to take one day other than Sunday off; so when his business became healthy enough, he announced he was taking Mondays off.

To Laurie, this was heaven. She looked forward to their getting a baby-sitter and spending the day together, or having Ike watch the kids while she spent the day shopping and running errands. She had felt so isolated and trapped that she couldn't wait to get away for a few hours.

There was a breakdown in communication the first time Ike took a Monday off. He agreed to watch the kids for a while, and she assumed he knew she would be gone most of the day. Many of his clients had not gotten the word of his day off; so he was trying to answer calls and do business over the phone while keeping track of the kids. The longer Laurie was gone, the angrier Ike became.

When she got home, he gave her an earful. Not only was she not going to have a free baby-sitter on his next day off, but he was also going golfing all day. His day off, in case she didn't know it, was for his sake, not hers, and that was the way things were going to be.

"When do I get a day off?" she said. That was a valid question, of course, but it was a mistake to ask just then.

"You get a day off all day every day," he said. He lived to regret that foolish remark.

When tempers cooled, the Vanderays knew they had a problem. Ike established on his voice mail that he was unavailable Mondays. He pledged to baby-sit from breakfast through lunch so Laurie could eat out with friends and get her errands and shopping done. She agreed to let him do whatever he wanted in the afternoon, and if she needed a baby-sitter so she could go with him or remain out on her own, that was okay. Monday evenings also became their date nights.

"That revolutionized our marriage," Ike says. "I feel I'm helping her. I get time to have some fun. She's happier because she gets out, sometimes for the whole day and evening. And even though we're each freer to do what we want, we are also seeing more of each other than ever."

Laurie says Ike seems like the same young, energetic, funny, creative guy she married. "He's less uptight, and we have fun like we used to. We talk like never before. Sometimes we go somewhere before or after dinner, but often we don't. Sometimes we close the restaurant, gabbing and planning and telling each other everything all evening. We've even been known to go and park!"

FRITZ AND PAIGE JOHNSTON

I was privileged to work with Fritz and Paige Johnston on a lengthy magazine article about their marriage. I met Fritz in the early 1990s when he was a college basketball coach.

At the time of the crisis, Fritz was near the top of his profession—a Division One coach admired and sought after, a speaker, a jogger—in short, the envy of many other wives. Only Paige knew the truth. He was invisible at home, wrapped up in his work, his speaking engagements, and his physical fitness. Paige was treated as "the little woman" who was to handle the home and provide the ideal environment for him so he could remain at the top of his game.

A depth of spirituality and character marks Paige and precluded her looking for another man and even eliminated from her mind the possibility of divorcing Fritz when their troubles arose. She admits, however, that she was terribly vulnerable during the crisis and can't say with certainty that she could have fought off the urge to look to someone else if certain circumstances had been in place.

Fritz thought he had a good marriage. His wife was beautiful and talented and a good mother. She was a creative decorator, a good cook, a singer—in short, everything a man like Fritz could want in a wife.

For years Paige had tried to get Fritz's attention. Her methods became more and more drastic as his solutions to her tantrums became more and more predictable. If she crabbed about his lack of attention or demanded to know why he ignored her in public, if she complained about his curtness to her or his condescension, or if she wanted to know why he never touched her except in bed or didn't have time to talk to her for even ten minutes a day, he would quickly take the temperature of the situation. If it looked serious he would apologize, make promises, bring her flowers, take her out to dinner, and see how long that kept her happy.

After six years she had had it, and he didn't even suspect

it. She dropped the bomb on him one Sunday afternoon in December. He had killed her emotionally, she said. She told him she would not divorce him, would not leave him, but that neither could she guarantee any emotional response to him whatsoever. He had killed every last vestige of love she'd ever felt for him. She was finished, defeated, deflated, and she couldn't even smile.

It was as if someone had kicked him in the stomach. When he started his promise to turn over a new leaf, she simply went upstairs to bed. He knew this was serious and that no bandage was going to make things right again. He wept, sensing, knowing finally that she was right. He begged for forgiveness from God and for a solution.

Fritz was an obsessive, compulsive person, driven to succeed at whatever he set his mind to, whether it meant working out for hours, building a winning basketball team, or speaking a hundred times a year. He could do anything. And now he decided to put his mind to his marriage. He was ready and willing to do whatever it took not just to salvage it, but to make it the best it could be. He wept and wept as God brought to his mind dozens of things he should have done over the years. He was reminded of every complaint Paige had registered over the decades, and he filled page after page of a yellow legal pad, determined to change his ways on every point.

God also led him to a book, *Love Life for Every Married Couple* by Ed Wheat, and he memorized the principles that urged him to apply the BEST acronym. He was to bless, edify, share, and touch his wife constantly, not just to win her back but also simply because it was the right thing to do. In fact, Dr. Wheat stipulated in his book that all this activity would not guarantee any response from the hurting spouse. He said in essence that the wounded partner may never respond after all the damage that had been done, but these principles applied anyway and should be followed.

Fritz was desperate to convince Paige that this was no typical restart. He meant it this time. He had really heard her. He loved her with all his heart and wanted to prove it. He was so committed to his marriage that everything else in his life paled in comparison, and yet she could not bring herself to respond. She couldn't smile or even speak except in cordial, formal, functional conversation. He got no encouragement and said, "I felt as if I were looking into the eyes of a dead woman, a woman I had killed."

The story continues, of course, and happily. Eventually Fritz proved himself. God forgave him and has given him the strength to maintain his commitment to this day. Paige finally forgave him and saw life and love return to her being. At the time of their marital crisis they had two children. They have since had two more.

A miraculous transformation has taken place in that home, all because Fritz got the message and planted hedges, albeit almost too late.

He talks to his wife a lot every day.

He spends time with her and with the children. He remembers special days.

They date frequently.

He applies a lot of nonsexual touching.

She has become the center of his life.

It hasn't been a quick fix. He knows he can never let his guard down, never slip into the old patterns. Now that he is head coach of an even bigger college basketball program and the family has moved to another state, the risks and temptations are greater than ever. Yet his resolve is all the stronger. Remember, these were not just leaves he turned over. They were hedges he planted deep in thick, rich soil, and they're growing strong.

OTHER HEDGES

Have you ever noticed yourself taking your wife for granted? Maybe you're a funny guy, charming, a storyteller. But she's heard them all. You don't come alive until you have a new audience. At a party you give people eye contact, really listen, use your best humor and your most charming qualities. Try treating your wife the way you would someone you just met.

Scripture is clear that we are to prefer others as more important than ourselves. The Bible says, "Let nothing be done through selfish ambition or conceit, but in lowliness of mind let each esteem others better than himself. Let each of you look out not only for his own interests, but also for the interests of others" (Philippians 2:3-4).

Imagine the impact on your marriage and family if you practiced that at home. Charm your wife. Amuse her. Tell her your best stories. Give her the details from your office that you might otherwise have saved for when you have the floor in a social situation. Look at her, smile at her, wink at her, make it obvious she's your favorite person in the world, not just in the room. And do this when you're alone too.

Some couples schedule a breakfast out each week. I know a pastor and two business executives who have regular appointments with their wives booked right onto their calendars, and their assistants know those dates are inviolable.

They don't feel obligated to tell callers where their boss will be, but they do say, "I'm sorry. That slot is filled."

To a busy man, a regular appointment with his wife is every bit as much of a hedge as the rest of mine are. Spend time talking with your wife. Find out what her deepest needs are, what she really wants and requires from you. Then plant a hedge around that, around her, around you, around your marriage. It'll be the best gardening you've ever done.

STUDY GUIDE

By John Perrodin

INTRODUCTION

"No trespassing" should be the sign on every man and woman's heart when it comes to the relationship God has given him or her to protect, honor, and cherish.

Psalm 89:40 implies that strongholds are brought to ruin when hedges are broken down. Job 1:10 implies that Job was so richly blessed—before God allowed him to be tested—because God had made a hedge "around him, around his household, and around all that he ha[d] on every side."

Jesus told parables about landowners who planted vineyards and protected them with hedges. When those hedges were trampled or removed, ruin came to the precious possessions of those landowners.

People are much more precious than land or holdings. If we can keep from deceiving ourselves about our own resolve and inner strength, we will see the need for healthy hedges that keep love in and infidelity out.

THE TANGLED WEB

MAINTAINING THE HEDGES AROUND YOUR HEART

John and Sue convinced themselves that their love was so perfect, God had to be in it. That is often the basis for an affair. God wants us to be happy, you may hear. Ironic then, isn't it, how often we hear that the supposed perfect couple can't hold things together? They've vaunted happiness above fidelity, selfishness over commitment.

TAKE ACTION

Take steps now to keep from losing focus on what first attracted you to your spouse. Write to your beloved, setting out what excited, interested, and delighted you about her. Accentuate the positive—no negative or corrective comments. Affirm and encourage your spouse. Put your thoughts in a card, and slip it under a pillow or post it someplace she'll be sure to find it.

NURTURING THE HEDGES OF YOUR HOME

Maybe on a business trip you hung around with a colleague of the opposite sex, and upon reflection you wouldn't have wanted your spouse to do the same. Maybe nothing improper was said or done, but investing the emotional energy and time was inappropriate.

For a hedge to grow, it needs the proper nutrients at the right time. Gardening requires patience, skill, and creativity. Without understanding specific needs it's impossible to nurture anyone in a meaningful way.

TALK IT OUT

1. Put yourself in your spouse's place. Does she struggle with depression? Temptation? Exhaustion? Anger? Fear?

2. How do you cultivate intimacy outside the bedroom? How do you show you care?

3. How can you grow emotional attachments to your spouse?

4. How do you stay close to the one you've married through secret signs, knowing looks, and special touches?

PLANTING NEW HEDGES

John and Sue allowed themselves to admire, like, respect, and enjoy each other without giving a second thought to the progression of feelings, the danger of developing emotional attachments, the lure of infatuation. Consider why this was such a problem.

TALK IT OUT

1. Have you ever downgraded your spouse, even in jest, to another? Why? When? How did you feel? Did you bring up your concerns to your partner?

2. What hedge could you build to protect your marriage? Talk over your answer with your spouse.

3. Have you or your spouse ever contemplated giving up? What pushed you to the limit?

4. How has no-fault divorce changed the way people think? Is it too easy to divorce today?

5. What hedge do you need to strengthen your relationship?

COUNTING THE COST OF IGNORING HEDGES

Couples committed for life are oddities today. But lifelong commitment should still be our goal . . . even if it's a tough one.

Fortunately, we can learn solid lessons from others, benefiting from their strengths and weaknesses. We don't have to make mistakes if we can glean from the errors of those who have gone before us. To Christians, divorce should always be seen as the last possible option. But it helps to discuss the subject in order to better understand what is causing pain in a relationship. Or what has killed someone else's.

Consider the unwilling participants in the marriage feast from Luke 14:15-24:

> Now when one of those who sat at the table with Him heard these things, he said to Him, "Blessed is he who shall eat bread in the kingdom of God!" Then He said to him, "A certain man gave a great supper and invited many, and sent his servant at supper time to say to those who were invited, 'Come, for all things are now ready.'
>
> "But they all with one accord began to make excuses. The first said to him, 'I have bought a piece of ground, and I must go and see it. I ask you to have me excused.' And another said, 'I have bought five yoke of oxen, and I am going to test them. I ask you to have me excused.' Still another said, 'I have married a wife, and therefore I cannot come.'
>
> "So that servant came and reported these things to his master. Then the master of the house, being angry, said to his servant, 'Go out quickly into the streets and lanes of the city, and bring in here the poor and the maimed and the lame and

the blind.' And the servant said, 'Master, it is done as you commanded, and still there is room.'

"Then the master said to the servant, 'Go out into the highways and hedges, and compel them to come in, that my house may be filled. For I say to you that none of those men who were invited shall taste my supper.'"

Couples often neglect what God has in store for them. They reject the hope of tomorrow for today's dalliance. While we know that the union between husband and wife is a holy estate, we treat it as a bother, a hassle, an old garment easily cast off. Rediscover the gift in your relationship.

TAKE ACTION

If so many of your friends and acquaintances have fallen—people you never would have suspected—how will *you* avoid being a casualty? Talk and pray with your spouse about how you will avoid being one more statistic. List five reasons you want to experience a life-long marriage and then five steps you can take toward marital longevity.

THE CHANGING CLIMATE

MAINTAINING THE HEDGES AROUND YOUR HEART

Recognizing danger keeps you on the path to victory. Acknowledge infatuation for what it is. Too many Christians deny it. In the workplace it's common to meet someone with whom there seems an immediate bonding. You can be married for years and still develop a crush on someone. You like them, they like you, you hit it off. That is the time to deal with the problem, before it can become a serious dilemma. That's why hedges are so important.

TAKE ACTION

In the last twenty years alone, several evangelical leaders have fallen prey to sexual temptation. But so have many lesser-known leaders, perhaps someone in your own church. Work with your spouse to come up with a list of ten ways society and morals have changed over the past two decades. Discuss why these changes make it harder than ever to stay faithful. Talk about how the Body of Christ deals with such disclosures.

NURTURING THE HEDGES OF YOUR HOME

Don't treat a new friend of the opposite sex the way you treat an old, respected friend. Refrain from touching her, being alone with her, flirting with her (even in jest), or saying anything to her you wouldn't say if your spouse were there. Conversely, friendships with long-admired associates can quickly turn into something more intimate.

Be careful of relationships with members of the opposite sex. Appropriate hedges can help guard against temptation.

TALK IT OUT

1. Discuss the concept of "instant attraction." Has it ever happened to you?

2. What can you do if you feel that surge or charge when you met someone new?

3. What triggers your interest in someone of the opposite sex?

4. How would you define your and your spouse's traditional roles?

. . . creative roles?

. . . changing roles?

5. Who prepares the most meals?

6. Who cleans the house most often?

7. Who fixes the car and mows the lawn?

8. Who cares for the children?

9. Who initiates intimacy?

PLANTING NEW HEDGES

We must plant hedges well in advance of even meeting someone else. It's the painless way to protect your marriage. Hedges nip marriage-threatening relationships before they get started.

It's her turn now. Women in record numbers are cheating on their husbands. Why? They are often ignored by busy husbands. Many women throw themselves into their work and find companionship with lonely, unattached men—unless well-tended hedges are in place.

TALK IT OUT

1. What modern opportunities can be marriage-killers?

2. List common interests that allow you and your spouse to share not only quality time but also quantity time.

3. What do you think about married couples having separate vacations, separate interests, and separate beds?

4. What hedge do you need to plant and nurture to strengthen your relationship?

COUNTING THE COST OF IGNORING HEDGES

A man with as perfect a wife as he could ever want is still capable of lust, of a senseless seeking of that which would destroy him and his family. If he does not fear his own potential and construct a hedge around himself and his marriage, he heads for disaster.

Consider the story of Joseph from Genesis 39:1-15:

Now Joseph had been taken down to Egypt. And Potiphar, an officer of Pharaoh, captain of the guard, an Egyptian, bought him from the Ishmaelites who had taken him down there. The LORD was with Joseph, and he was a successful man; and he was in the house of his master the Egyptian.

And his master saw that the LORD was with him and that the LORD made all he did to prosper in his hand. So Joseph found favor in his sight, and served him. Then he made him overseer of his house, and all that he had he put under his authority.

So it was, from the time that he had made him overseer of his house and all that he had, that the LORD blessed the Egyptian's house for Joseph's sake; and the blessing of the LORD was on all that he had in the house and in the field. Thus he left all that he had in Joseph's hand, and he did not know what he had except for the bread which he ate.

Now Joseph was handsome in form and appearance. And it came to pass after these things that his master's wife cast longing eyes on Joseph, and she said, "Lie with me."

But he refused and said to his master's wife, "Look, my master does not know what is with me in the house, and he has committed all that he has to my hand. There is no one greater in this house than I, nor has he kept back anything from me but you, because you are his wife. How then can I do this great wickedness, and sin against God?"

So it was, as she spoke to Joseph day by day, that he did not heed her, to lie with her or to be with her. But it happened about this time, when Joseph went into the house to do his work, and none of the men of the house was inside, that she caught him by his garment, saying, "Lie with me."

But he left his garment in her hand, and fled and ran outside. And so it was, when she saw that he had left his garment in her hand and fled outside, that she called to the men of her house and spoke to them, saying, "See, he has brought in to us a Hebrew to mock us. He came in to me to lie with me, and I cried out with a loud voice. And it happened, when he heard that I lifted my voice and cried out, that he left his garment with me, and fled and went outside."

Temptation can overwhelm us before we know it. Our only hope is to run. Second Timothy 2:22 says, "Flee also youthful lusts . . ." Beware the not-so-youthful lusts as well.

ACTION POINT

Only by understanding mutual weaknesses can a husband and wife truly help each other overcome the shame and pain. Confess to your spouse privately your personal points of temptation. Be blunt about your struggles. Pray together for strength. Talk about what makes it easier (or more difficult) to resist temptation.

DON'T BLAME GOD

MAINTAINING THE HEDGES AROUND YOUR HEART

Understanding how God made us is crucial. As a child, Jerry found he had a powerful interest in the opposite sex. He writes, "Had I only known this was normal! That I was not alone! That such attraction to women, yes, even to their sexuality, was God's idea! Is that heresy? It's not now, and it wasn't then. Though I can't recall having purely lustful thoughts in junior high, I carried a deep sense of guilt about even wanting to look at girls."

Some things never change. Men are grown-up boys, each with varying abilities to withstand the lure of an attractive female. Some stop and stare. Others know better. Pretending we don't notice is neither healthy nor helpful.

TAKE ACTION

Celebrate your differences. Is the adage that opposites attract true for you? Talk and pray with your spouse about the ways that you are the same as well as different. Find common ground in interests, likes/dislikes, and dreams for the future. Categorize your differences so you can better discern and respect your individual preferences.

NURTURING THE HEDGES OF YOUR HOME

Sex is a gift from God. He created men and women to be drawn to each other. "I know some people may laugh at my notion of looking at women to appreciate God's creativity and would accuse me of inventing a spiritual reason to leer. I maintain that after years of steeling myself to avert my eyes from something made attractive by God, developing an appreciation for it is far healthier." Jerry expresses an honest desire to keep his promise of purity to his wife. But he also knows he will sometimes see beauty that begs a second look. Thankfully, that doesn't have to be the same as lust.

TALK IT OUT

1. Deal with the double standard we all know exists. What happens when a man sees that others have noticed his wife? How does a woman respond to someone else's untoward interest in her husband?

2. How did God make you? What thrills and delights you?

3. How do you communicate your likes/dislikes to your spouse?

4. Describe a chauvinist you've known. How do you differ from the stereotypical male? How are you the same?

5. How do you teach your kids about sex? What's your style?

PLANTING NEW HEDGES

"I have been quick to point out to my sons that the rush of feeling they might experience for a beautiful woman should never be mistaken for true love," Jerry writes. "Such a rush is a mere infatuation, physical and sensual attraction, a path to a dead end. A relationship may begin with physical attraction, but to build on that alone leads to disaster." Jerry makes the point that any relationship based purely on appearance is shallow and ultimately meaningless. Man looks at the outward appearance, but God sees the heart. If we exalt appearance over substance, we pervert the natural attraction between the sexes that God planned.

TALK IT OUT

1. Why can a long-lasting relationship never be based solely on physical attraction?

2. What do you do to keep the passion in your relationship?

3. Talk about how nonsexual touching can improve a marriage.

4. What hedge do you need to plant and nurture to strengthen your relationship?

COUNTING THE COST OF IGNORING HEDGES

Women need to understand how their dress, appearance, and attitude affects the opposite sex. Women and men take different routes to excitement and eroticism. As Jerry explains it, "These differences in attraction actually compete with each other. A man is turned on by the mere thought of a beautiful woman—imagining, fantasizing about the possibilities. When he meets a woman, the scenario has already been played out in his mind." The woman, however, needs time and attention. She can't be rushed. The bottom line is: Men and women are not from the same planet. We don't even speak the same language.

Consider the story of Abigail, a life-saving wife found in 1 Samuel 25:14-25:

> Now one of the young men told Abigail, Nabal's wife, saying, "Look, David sent messengers from the wilderness to greet our master; and he reviled them. But the men were very good to us, and we were not hurt, nor did we miss anything as long as we accompanied them, when we were in the fields. They were a wall to us both by night and day, all the time we were with them keeping the sheep. Now therefore, know and consider what you will do, for harm is determined against our master and against all his household. For he is such a scoundrel that one cannot speak to him."
>
> Then Abigail made haste and took two hundred loaves of bread, two skins of wine, five sheep already dressed, five seahs of roasted grain, one hundred clusters of raisins, and two hundred cakes of figs, and loaded them on donkeys. And she said to her servants, "Go on before me; see, I am coming after you." But she did not tell her husband Nabal. So it was, as she rode on the donkey, that she went down under cover of the hill; and there were David and his men, coming down toward her, and she met them.
>
> Now David had said, "Surely in vain I have protected all that this fellow has in the wilderness, so that nothing was missed of all that belongs to him. And he has repaid me evil for good. May God do so, and more also, to the enemies of David, if I leave one male of all who belong to him by morning light."
>
> Now when Abigail saw David, she dismounted quickly from the donkey, fell on her face before David, and bowed down to the ground. So she fell at his feet and said: "On me, my lord, on me let this iniquity be! And please let your maidservant speak in your ears, and hear the words of your maidservant. Please, let not my lord regard this scoundrel Nabal. For as his name is, so is he: Nabal is his name, and folly is with him! But I, your maidservant, did not see the young men of my lord whom you sent.

TAKE ACTION

Make this a no-holds-barred discussion. Discuss whether Abigail fits the mold of the submissive wife. Was she faithful to her husband or merely concerned about her own skin? Share ways you've come to your spouse's rescue. Talk about how you cover for each other. Highlight your wife's strengths, and contrast them with your weaknesses.

Study Guide for Chapter 4

THE DYNAMICS OF FLIRTATION

MAINTAINING THE HEDGES AROUND YOUR HEART

Though flirting seems harmless, it can be both wrong and dangerous. "If someone says something flirtatious to me," Jerry writes, "my first impulse is to expand on it, play with it, see how quick and funny I can be. But I resist that. It isn't fair. It's mental and emotional unfaithfulness. I would be exercising a portion of my brain and soul reserved for my exclusive lover." Our time and energy should go toward keeping our own relationship vibrant, not diffused and diverted by flirting with someone else.

TAKE ACTION

How does your wife respond if you bring her flowers? How does it impact you if she sends you a love note? Talk about how such gestures make you both feel. Explore ways you can love without ulterior motives—including the expectation of sex. List unexpected things you could do to show your spouse you're still in love. Hints: Take the kids to the library so she can take a nap; make breakfast in bed; have a gift delivered.

Suggested assignment: perform three such random acts of love this week.

NURTURING THE HEDGES OF YOUR HOME

If you want to flirt, flirt with your spouse. She may not look, feel, or sound the way she did when you first flirted with her years ago. She may not know what to think at first. But your partner still wants to flirt. Try it. Wink at her across the room. Blow her a kiss no one else sees. Play footsie under the table. Give a squeeze, a pinch, a tickle no one else notices. You'll be glad you did.

TALK IT OUT

1. How do you define flirting?
2. How did you flirt with your spouse before you married?
3. On your honeymoon?
4. How do you flirt with her now?
5. Discuss why flirting has become less frequent and less important.

PLANTING NEW HEDGES

Married couples do not commonly flirt with each other, so this may have to be relearned. Marital flirting is really no different than adolescent flirting. You can do the same things, only everything you're thinking about and hoping will come of it is legal, normal, acceptable, and beautiful. Marital flirting is fun and safe. You can tease your wife about something you'd like to do later—and follow through. What could be more fun?

TALK IT OUT

1. Discuss the difference between a crush or infatuation and love.

2. Talk about when you've been concerned that someone had a crush on you or your spouse.

3. How did you handle that uncomfortable feeling?

4. Share a story about an adolescent crush. Do you feel the same rush when you think about your spouse?

5. What hedge do you need to plant and nurture to strengthen your relationship?

COUNTING THE COST OF IGNORING HEDGES

Flirting always starts out fun, funny, and innocent. "I know two men who have left their wives for other men's wives, and it all began with what each party thought was harmless flirting," Jerry writes. There's no such thing, unless you're flirting with your spouse.

As with any other innocent activity that eventually gets out of hand, flirting can be a good and natural part of a person's progression toward true love. God made us able to respond emotionally and physically to attention from the opposite sex, and that is the initial aim of flirting. But like any of His gifts, this is one that can be cheapened and counterfeited, used for evil as well as for good.

Consider this advice from Proverbs 5:15-20:

> Drink water from your own cistern, and running water from your own well. Should your fountains be dispersed abroad, streams of water in the streets? Let them be only your own, and not for strangers with you. Let your fountain be blessed, and rejoice with the wife of your youth.
>
> As a loving deer and a graceful doe, let her breasts satisfy you at all times; and always be enraptured with her love. For why should you, my son, be enraptured by an immoral woman, and be embraced in the arms of a seductress?

TAKE ACTION

Temptation comes in every shape and size. Often we don't even see it coming. Unburden yourself. Discuss the temptations in your life, at work, at home, on the road. Share heart to heart the concerns you have about family, friends, or coworkers who push the line of propriety. If you have acted inappropriately, talk to your spouse about the situation and how you can avoid it in the future. You long ago made a sacred vow to remain pure for your spouse. Write that promise as you remember it.

Study Guide for Chapter 5

THE BIBLICAL BASIS FOR HEDGES

MAINTAINING THE HEDGES AROUND YOUR HEART

Adulterers are liars, and they are as good at it as alcoholics are. Jerry tells an anecdote about an acquaintance who told him that he was seeing a woman other than his wife, but that they were just friends. He was not, he claimed, interested in her romantically. They had a lot in common, talked easily, and liked each other's company. Jerry told him he didn't have the right to have a woman as a close friend when he was married and that it was slowly killing his wife. The man seemed convinced and convicted of his sin.

TAKE ACTION

It's tragic to watch the death of a marriage. List some of the high-profile figures you've heard of whose love life has been grist for supermarket tabloids. What is it about relationships in a fishbowl that are so difficult? Consider how you and your spouse are watched by children, family, coworkers, and friends. Discuss ways you can set an example of purity and faithfulness that will have a lasting impact on others.

NURTURING THE HEDGES OF YOUR HOME

Jerry says his friend seemed to see the light, even promised he would break off the relationship. But that very night he met the woman after work. They embraced, kissing, before they left the state in her car. By the time he really came to his senses and pleaded for his wife to take him back—he missed his four boys terribly—the divorce was final. Adultery causes chaos. It's inevitable.

TALK IT OUT

1. What does Jerry mean when he says, "The escape comes with the temptation. It's preventative medicine, not first aid after you've already set your course on a path toward injury"?

2. How do children respond to divorce? Are they resilient, as some so-called experts claim?

3. What are your personal limits of forgiveness? Could you ever forgive your spouse for being unfaithful? Why or why not?

PLANTING NEW HEDGES

As much as television, movies, and videos try to convince us otherwise, adultery is not funny. And even though it has become common, it's certainly not normal from God's point of view. The media has convinced many that adultery is hardly more serious than exceeding the speed limit. "Everybody does it." "This is a new age." "Don't be so old-fashioned." "Get with the program." That is the message we too often hear.

TALK IT OUT

1. It is often said that married couples have better and more frequent sex than live-ins. Why would or should this be true?

2. Discuss the new world of adultery of the mind. Today's temptations come in the form of films, books, magazines, TV shows, comics, music, and more online options than we can list. Talk about ways you can overcome the desire to mentally stray.

3. Why does God forbid adultery? What does that say about the marital relationship?

4. What hedge do you need to plant and nurture to strengthen your relationship?

COUNTING THE COST OF IGNORING HEDGES

Why is it so important that couples avoid adultery? Why does Jerry insist that we must build hedges around our hearts, eyes, hands, spouses, and marriages? If the Bible puts adultery in the same class as murder, it is a threat not only to our marriages, but also to our very lives.

Consider the admonition to walk in love as found in Ephesians 5:1-7.

> Therefore be imitators of God as dear children. And walk in love, as Christ also has loved us and given Himself for us, an offering and a sacrifice to God for a sweet-smelling aroma.
>
> But fornication and all uncleanness or covetousness, let it not even be named among you, as is fitting for saints; neither filthiness, nor foolish talking, nor coarse jesting, which are not fitting, but rather giving of thanks.
>
> For this you know, that no fornicator, unclean person, nor covetous man, who is an idolater, has any inheritance in the kingdom of Christ and God. Let no one deceive you with empty words, for because of these things the wrath of God comes upon the sons of disobedience. Therefore do not be partakers with them.

TAKE ACTION

Define "filthiness," "foolish talking," and "coarse jesting." How are loose words connected with flirting and, ultimately, adultery? If purity is the goal of every believer, what are we doing to move closer to holiness? Create your own list of ways you and your wife can draw closer to God.

THE POWER OF SELF-DECEPTION

MAINTAINING THE HEDGES AROUND YOUR HEART

The key is preventative maintenance. Once that first step has been taken down the road of self-deceit and rationalization, there is no turning back. Each excuse sounds more plausible, and before he knows it, the typical male has satisfied every curiosity, every urge. Regardless of the remorse, the self-loathing, and the pledges for the future, the pattern will repeat itself as long as he refuses to flee. There is no other defense, no other option.

TAKE ACTION

It's prayer time . . . finally. Amazingly, couples often feel they're too busy to pray. But unless you both are connected to God, you can't help but sputter and falter as you seek to build your home on Him. Discuss your top three reasons why it's tough to pray together as a couple. Discuss ways to get past these, and end your discussion with prayer.

NURTURING THE HEDGES OF YOUR HOME

No one likes to admit weakness. We'd all like to know someone so spiritual, so wise, so disciplined that he could ignore or throw away a porn magazine left in a hotel room by the previous guest. Jerry admits that if he didn't throw it out upon first discovering it, ignoring it would be a chore. We don't all share the same trigger points, but we need to acknowledge our problem areas.

TALK IT OUT

1. Discuss why couples carefully construct facades rather than looking at each other eye-to-eye.

2. Can we really hide who we are from ourselves, others, God? Why do we keep trying to do just that?

3. What's your prayer history? Have you received powerful answers to prayer that should encourage you to continue?

4. List some Christian prayer warriors you admire, and explain why.

PLANTING NEW HEDGES

"I need to plant hedges against being alone or working too closely with women I simply admire or like," Jerry writes. "That, to me, is more dangerous. I could see myself becoming attached to or enamored with someone I worked with if I didn't emphasize keeping everything on a professional basis."

TALK IT OUT

1. Is there anything wrong with admiring someone of the opposite sex? Are friendships among adults of the opposite sex possible outside the phony world of TV?

2. List your personal hedges to keep business relationships on a professional level. Does your place of employment have standards on this issue? If not, what should they be?

3. Do you find yourself jealous of your spouse's relation-

ships? Talk about what would make you feel more (or less) comfortable about them.

4. What hedge do you need to plant and nurture to strengthen your relationship?

COUNTING THE COST OF IGNORING HEDGES

The only future in self-deceit is ruin. Let's quit kidding ourselves. We sometimes have filthy thoughts. No, we don't have to broadcast every base notion and urge to the public, but in our heart of hearts let's avoid denial. Who are we to think we are above carnal drives and desires?

Consider John 3:19-21:

> And this is the condemnation, that the light has come into the world, and men loved darkness rather than light, because their deeds were evil. For everyone practicing evil hates the light and does not come to the light, lest his deeds should be exposed. But he who does the truth comes to the light, that his deeds may be clearly seen, that they have been done in God.

Now think about how this relates to Romans 7:14-16:

> For we know that the law is spiritual, but I am carnal, sold under sin. For what I am doing, I do not understand. For what I will to do, that I do not practice; but what I hate, that I do. If, then, I do what I will not to do, I agree with the law that it is good.

TAKE ACTION

You can't be helped until you admit you need help. Take time to share with your spouse your weakness regarding sexual temptations. Be honest and open. List problem areas. Discuss your concerns, and get her help, accountability, and prayer support. If necessary, consider meeting together with your pastor or a Christian counselor.

TWO'S COMPANY; THREE'S SECURITY

MAINTAINING THE HEDGES AROUND YOUR HEART

Jerry's philosophy is that if you take care of how things look, you take care of how they are. Logic says that if we are following the biblical injunction to abstain from even the appearance of evil (see 1 Thessalonians 5:22, KJV), we will also abstain from the evil itself. Meetings with the opposite sex should only take place in public or with at least one other person present. That provides protection for everyone involved, first for their reputations and finally against temptation.

TAKE ACTION

Abstaining from even the appearance of evil has fallen into disfavor in certain Christian circles. Many prefer to dwell on their freedoms rather than hemming themselves in. Work with your spouse to develop a workable policy on how each of you should interact with unrelated members of the opposite sex. Consider what limits would make you both comfortable and keep you from violating each other's sensibilities.

NURTURING THE HEDGES OF YOUR HOME

Once Jerry found, at the last minute, that his business travel plans included flying on the same plane and staying in the same hotel as a female employee. Had he known earlier he would have made other plans. "With a phone call from the airport," Jerry writes, "I passed the buck to my wife. . . . The fact that I had called her and had made a practice of keeping her informed of such seeming improprieties for years gave her the confidence to immediately agree to the trip." It takes discipline, but we can set patterns of faithfulness that protect our marriages.

TALK IT OUT

1. Tell your spouse about times someone has made you feel uncomfortable or crossed an invisible line of intimacy.

2. Talk about why you would or would not keep such information to yourself.

3. If you ever feel your spouse doesn't recognize the signs of interest by the opposite sex, be ready to talk this out.

PLANTING NEW HEDGES

Jerry includes dining with unrelated members of the opposite sex as a prohibition. Why? Because there is something personal and even intimate about eating with someone. It's a time to relax, to sit close, to open up. If that weren't true, why are so many dates centered on food?

TALK IT OUT

1. Talk about the most romantic meal you've ever shared with your husband or wife. What made it special?

2. What is there about intimate conversation over a delicious dinner that opens your heart and soul to your companion? Discuss how such a setting might lower inhibitions and allow for inappropriate topics between coworkers or even strangers.

3. Suggest ways to keep your family close even when traveling. How can a man make his unavailability clear to someone he meets on a business trip?

4. What hedge do you need to plant and nurture to strengthen your relationship?

COUNTING THE COST OF IGNORING HEDGES

Dining and traveling hedges should never be trampled. It's easy to morph into someone we're not when away from home. The price of suspicion is high, and the price of infidelity is even higher.

Consider Ephesians 5:8-14. Note how it urges believers to walk in the light and to make sure that all they do is appropriate and above board:

> For you were once darkness, but now you are light in the Lord. Walk as children of light (for the fruit of the Spirit is in all goodness, righteousness, and truth), finding out what is acceptable to the Lord. And have no fellowship with the unfruitful works of darkness, but rather expose them.
>
> For it is shameful even to speak of those things which are done by them in secret. But all things that are exposed are made manifest by the light, for whatever makes manifest is light. Therefore He says:
>
> *"Awake, you who sleep,*
> *Arise from the dead,*
> *And Christ will give you light."*

TAKE ACTION

Plan an intimate dinner for two. Work on the details together, find child care, and create a completely romantic mini-getaway where you and your spouse can relax and talk. Make it a priority to discuss what you mean to each other. Leave problems out of the picture. Make this a time of sanctuary for just the two of you.

Study Guide for Chapter 8

TOUCHY, TOUCHY!

MAINTAINING THE HEDGES AROUND YOUR HEART

"If I embrace only dear friends or relatives and only in the presence of others, I am not even tempted to make the embrace longer or more impassioned than is appropriate," Jerry writes. "I like hugging women. It's fun, and it can be friendly. But if I allowed myself to embrace just anyone, even dear friends, in private, I would be less confident of my motives and my subsequent actions." Humans need companionship. That's why the power of touch can be so overwhelming.

TAKE ACTION

Come up with a list of socially appropriate, non-tactile ways to show friendship or affection. Put more simply: How can you show you care about someone of the opposite sex without resorting to hugs or actions that could send mixed messages? Also note which of these you use with your spouse and consider whether you should find more loving ways of communicating as husband and wife.

NURTURING THE HEDGES OF YOUR HOME

Touching and being touched, embracing and being embraced is as much a matter of common sense and decency as it is of ethnic background and custom. Because of the way Jerry was raised, he treads carefully in this area. If it doesn't happen to be an issue with you, Jerry recommends only that you be sensitive to the attitudes and interpretations of those you choose to touch. Others may have weaknesses you can't sense.

TALK IT OUT

1. Talk about your life as a child. Were your parents affectionate and open with hugs, kisses, and caresses?

2. With regard to physical affection, what kind of a home have you created for your spouse and children?

3. What are the good and bad aspects of being physically affectionate with people outside your family?

PLANTING NEW HEDGES

It's not always appropriate to embrace even a Christian of the opposite sex. For some, such openness to touching and hugging can be a problem. Jerry knows stories of people who fell in love because they enjoyed and looked forward to what began as a spiritual expression of brotherly and sisterly love. Don't open yourself to such a possibility.

TALK IT OUT

1. When you get together with your church family do you openly show affection? Does such sharing ever cross the line of appropriateness?

2. Do some have difficulty separating the positive feeling of a hug from the sexual connotation that sometimes accom-

panies it? Discuss how we, as Christians, should be especially careful that we don't make a weaker brother or sister fall.

3. Talk about how you feel about the new openness to physical affection we often see in church. Has this been a positive change? Why or why not?

4. What hedge do you need to plant and nurture to strengthen your relationship?

COUNTING THE COST OF IGNORING HEDGES

Jerry talks about a friend who spent time in the arms of a friend's wife. What began as seemingly innocent consolation over serious personal problems became a passionate embrace. "My friend was not without fault," Jerry writes, "but he was weak and vulnerable. Once she had taken advantage of him, there was no turning back. A marriage ended, and an affair began. There was no future in it for either of them, but they still played it out." And it all began with a hug.

Consider Ephesians 5:15-21, where we see that God's expectation for us is that we'll walk in wisdom, not foolishness:

> See then that you walk circumspectly, not as fools but as wise, redeeming the time, because the days are evil. Therefore do not be unwise, but understand what the will of the Lord is. And do not be drunk with wine, in which is dissipation; but be filled with the Spirit, speaking to one another in psalms and hymns and spiritual songs, singing and making melody in your heart to the Lord, giving thanks always for all things to God the Father in the name of our Lord Jesus Christ, submitting to one another in the fear of God.

TAKE ACTION

Learn from a good example. Think of a couple who has a dynamic marriage, and identify what keeps their relationship fresh. Note what they do together and what they avoid. Commit to growing your own marital bond and making that connection even stronger. You and your spouse should tell each other what positive changes you'd like to make.

SOME COMPLIMENTS DON'T PAY

MAINTAINING THE HEDGES AROUND YOUR HEART

Husband and wife should meet each other's needs, and others should mind their own business. Protect the hedge of marital intimacy.

TAKE ACTION

It's time for a love note. Write your spouse a letter describing what attracts you. List inside a beautiful card what thrills you about your beloved, and slip it under a pillow or some other place she's sure to find it.

NURTURING THE HEDGES OF YOUR HOME

Jerry bases part of this hedge on his own reactions to how men talk to his wife. Dianna is tall, dark, and stunning—a head turner. "It makes me proud to see men do a double take when they see her," he writes. "If they keep staring, though, I stare right back until they notice that she's with me."

The surest way to ward off inappropriate come-ons and to protect your marriage is by openly acknowledging and proclaiming your love.

TALK IT OUT

1. List some things others appreciate about your spouse.

2. Tell how you make clear to "lookers" that your wife is taken.

3. Discuss ways you could affirm your spouse for her wit, attractiveness, and spiritual depth. Talk about how you would feel if you learned someone else was making similar compliments.

PLANTING NEW HEDGES

"For some reason," Jerry writes, "it does not bother me if a man comments on my wife's hair or makeup or clothes. But if he should say that she looks pretty or is gorgeous or beautiful, that is too personal. Interestingly, either kind of compliment makes her uncomfortable, but she agrees that the personal approach is worse." Be careful that compliments don't cross the line.

TALK IT OUT

1. Discuss compliments that border on being too personal. Talk about why general comments may be within bounds but personal affirmations can be inappropriate.

2. Why do some people seem at ease with compliments while others squirm?

3. What hedge do you need to plant and nurture to strengthen your relationship?

COUNTING THE COST OF IGNORING HEDGES

If we run off with another man's spouse—even if we do find more pleasure, more romance, more sex, and more of our ego needs fulfilled—there is still the real world to deal with. In fact, it may be more burdensome than the one we left because of the spousal maintenance and child-care expenses from the previous marriage. If nothing else, divorce can be financially crushing.

Consider the encouraging words in 1 Thessalonians 5:12-18:

> And we urge you, brethren, to recognize those who labor among you, and are over you in the Lord and admonish you, and to esteem them very highly in love for their work's sake. Be at peace among yourselves.
>
> Now we exhort you, brethren, warn those who are unruly, comfort the fainthearted, uphold the weak, be patient with all. See that no one renders evil for evil to anyone, but always pursue what is good both for yourselves and for all.
>
> Rejoice always, pray without ceasing, in everything give thanks; for this is the will of God in Christ Jesus for you.

If this is how we are to treat brothers and sisters in the body, how much more should we encourage and exhort our spouses to live for—and like—Jesus Christ? Note the emphasis on rejoicing. Honest encouragement is one of the best ways a husband or wife can lead a spouse to "pursue what is good."

TAKE ACTION

A difficult question: Are you more adept at criticism or compliments? Talk this over with your spouse. Explore why you're better at one than the other. Commit to improve how you offer praise and tender advice.

LOOKING DOWN THE BARREL OF A LOADED GUN

MAINTAINING THE HEDGES AROUND YOUR HEART

We've all seen it played out repeatedly. A man hides his true desires behind a cloak of humor. A little crisis, a little honesty, and suddenly years of innocent flirting blossoms into an affair. It all began supposedly harmlessly.

TAKE ACTION

Here's a chance to do some research. Make a date with your wife to go to the mall, a park, or some other high-traffic area. Hold hands, and look for high-quality examples of flirting. Differentiate between couples showing flirtatious affection and strangers trying to connect. Note differences in approach and attitude. Jot your findings, and determine what works and what doesn't.

NURTURING THE HEDGES OF YOUR HOME

Flattery, flirtation, suggestive jesting, and what we say to our own spouses are all shades of the same color. Words can thrill, delight, entice, and excite. Beware the power of the tongue.

1. Why is it so difficult to retract something you've said? Share examples of things you wish you'd never said.

2. When do you find yourself the most flirtatious? What prompts this, and how can it be discouraged?

3. Is there a line of appropriate commentary that should not be crossed even with your spouse?

PLANTING NEW HEDGES

"We give the lie to the charge that married couples who never fight are probably as miserable and phony as those who fight all the time," Jerry writes. "We love each other. We don't always agree, and we get on each other's nerves occasionally, but neither of us likes tension in the air. We compete to see who can apologize first and get things talked out. We follow the biblical injunction to never let the sun go down upon our wrath (Ephesians 4:26)." Dealing with difficulties today prevents greater pain tomorrow.

1. Do you follow the scriptural admonition to not let the sun go down on your anger? Discuss this policy and why it is advised.

2. Define a "healthy discussion" and how you know when you've crossed the line to a heated argument.

3. What do our children learn from us about the way to handle disagreements?

4. What ways have you found to make your apologies more meaningful? If you owe your spouse an apology, take the time to say what needs to be said now.

5. What hedge do you need to plant and nurture to strengthen your relationship?

COUNTING THE COST OF IGNORING HEDGES

The real danger of flirtation comes when you pretend to be teasing but you'd really love to do just what you're suggesting.

The recipient of the flirting may not suspect the truth behind the humor, but if she responds in kind, there is opportunity for misunderstanding—or real understanding.

Consider what the book of James says about the power of the tongue in 3:2-12:

> For we all stumble in many things. If anyone does not stumble in word, he is a perfect man, able also to bridle the whole body. Indeed, we put bits in horses' mouths that they may obey us, and we turn their whole body. Look also at ships: although they are so large and are driven by fierce winds, they are turned by a very small rudder wherever the pilot desires.
>
> Even so the tongue is a little member and boasts great things. See how great a forest a little fire kindles! And the tongue is a fire, a world of iniquity. The tongue is so set among our members that it defiles the whole body, and sets on fire the course of nature; and it is set on fire by hell. For every kind of beast and bird, of reptile and creature of the sea, is tamed and has been tamed by mankind. But no man can tame the tongue.
>
> It is an unruly evil, full of deadly poison. With it we bless our God and Father, and with it we curse men, who have been made in the similitude of God. Out of the same mouth proceed blessings and cursing. My brethren, these things ought not to be so. Does a spring send forth fresh water and bitter from the same opening? Can a fig tree, my brethren, bear olives, or a grapevine bear figs? Thus, no spring can yield both salt water and fresh.

TAKE ACTION

The tongue is clearly an instrument for good or evil depending upon who is wielding the weapon. Put your recent research to use, and get down to some serious flirting with your spouse. Incorporate caring signs of affection into your daily relationship.

Study Guide for Chapter 11

MEMORIES

MAINTAINING THE HEDGES AROUND YOUR HEART

It may be naive to think that people would remain true to their vows just by repeating them frequently, but who knows? Jerry and Dianna have found this a healthy habit. It allows couples to better understand and reflect upon what they promised before God, friends, and each other.

TAKE ACTION

Find your wedding vows or a reasonable facsimile and recite them to your spouse. Look into her eyes, and add your own thoughts about why you feel especially blessed by your marriage.

NURTURING THE HEDGES OF YOUR HOME

Somehow, some way we need to ensure that we continue along the path of remaining true to our spouses. That means working on our weaknesses, shoring up our strengths, pouring our lives into each other. It's an effort, but it's also a privilege.

TALK IT OUT

1. Discuss how you lay down your life for your spouse and family. What could or should you do to make your love and affection even more obvious?

2. Why is it so difficult today for some to remain true to

their spouses? Share with each other your secrets for keeping the bond strong.

3. What is your spouse's greatest strength? Tell her what you most admire.

4. Explain why it's a good idea to repeat your vows to your spouse.

PLANTING NEW HEDGES

"I've never understood the long-standing double standard that seems to wink at males' infidelity while holding women in contempt for the same offense," Jerry writes. "Of course, the breaking of a sacred vow should not be tolerated for either sex." Vows are meant to be honored, becoming more solid and treasured over time.

TALK IT OUT

1. Discuss the double standard Jerry mentions. Why does there seem to be a growing tolerance for infidelity?

2. What would you do if a friend confessed unfaithfulness to you? What kind of advice would you give?

3. With all the opportunities for temptation online, talk about why the concept of an "affair" is broader now than it's ever been.

4. What would you do if you caught your spouse perusing pornography on the home computer?

5. What hedge do you need to plant and nurture to strengthen your relationship?

COUNTING THE COST OF IGNORING HEDGES

Adultery is devastating. Marriages that suffer this ultimate loss of trust can never really be the same. We can only imagine what a spouse who has taken back a partner who slept with another must go through to enjoy the marriage bed again.

As Ecclesiastes 2:10-11 says:

Whatever my eyes desired I did not keep from them.
I did not withhold my heart from any pleasure,
For my hear rejoiced in all my labor;
And this was my reward from all my labor.
Then I looked on al the works that my hands had done
And on the labor in which I had toiled;
And indeed all was vanity and grasping for the wind.
There was no profit under the sun.

TAKE ACTION

Write a letter together that you will one day give to your children, expressing why it's so important to value the wedding vows. Include both the text from your ceremony and comments that show why you're glad you've remained faithful through the years. This can become a special document you can present to your children on their wedding days.

QUALITY TIME VS. QUANTITY TIME

MAINTAINING THE HEDGES AROUND YOUR HEART

Children see a difference in a healthy marriage. "They know we're still affectionate and in love and demonstrative about it even after all these years," Jerry writes.

TAKE ACTION

Consider the broken and blended homes you're familiar with (maybe even your own), and talk about the "might have beens" if the original husband-and-wife bond had never been broken. Express to each other your commitment to keep your marriage strong. Pray together for protection of your relationship.

NURTURING THE HEDGES OF YOUR HOME

Strive to provide a model of love and caring and interdependence for your children. Show them what it means to make and keep a commitment, to set out on a lifetime of love with no wavering, no excuses, and no me-first philosophies. Your actions will speak volumes.

TALK IT OUT

1. Define true love. Discuss how your definition differs from what our culture calls love.

2. Talk about which commitments mean the most to you and why.

3. List how children benefit from seeing their parents love and care for one another.

4. Do you think a loving couple should ever discuss divorce? Why or why not?

PLANTING NEW HEDGES

"Hedges can do wonders for a family," Jerry writes, "and this policy of spending mega-blocks of time with the kids each day turned into rich benefits for Dianna and me too. Our time together was more relaxed, less hurried, less pressured, less obligatory." Children grow up so quickly. Unless we savor our time with them, one day we'll wake up regretting our selfishness.

TALK IT OUT

1. Explain the difference between quality and quantity time. Which is most important and why?

2. List your favorite things to do alone and with your spouse and family.

3. Discuss investing the time to put your family first. What would have to be sacrificed?

4. What things stress you the quickest? What relaxes you fastest? Talk these over with your spouse.

5. What hedge do you need to plant and nurture to strengthen your relationship?

COUNTING THE COST OF IGNORING HEDGES

Make a decision. Set a course. Carve out the time it takes to devote yourself to your wife and children. And plant a hedge that will protect you and her and them from the devastation of a broken home. Healthy hedges need time to grow.

Consider the famous passage from Ecclesiastes 3:1-8:

> *To everything there is a season,*
> *A time for every purpose under heaven:*
> *A time to be born,*
> *And a time to die;*
> *A time to plant,*
> *And a time to pluck what is planted;*
> *A time to kill,*
> *And a time to heal;*
> *A time to break down,*
> *And a time to build up;*
> *A time to weep,*
> *And a time to laugh;*
> *A time to mourn,*
> *And a time to dance;*
> *A time to cast away stones,*
> *And a time to gather stones;*
> *A time to embrace,*
> *And a time to refrain from embracing;*
> *A time to gain,*
> *And a time to lose;*
> *A time to keep,*
> *And a time to throw away;*
> *A time to tear,*
> *And a time to sew;*
> *A time to keep silence,*
> *And a time to speak;*
> *A time to love,*
> *And a time to hate;*
> *A time of war,*
> *And a time of peace.*

TAKE ACTION

Write your own version of Ecclesiastes 3:1-8. Express what the present time of life means for you and your family. It may represent diapers and potty training or perhaps driving lessons. Come up with a poignant, perhaps humorous analysis of "The State of Our Family."

Study Guide for Chapter 13

EVERYBODY LOVES A LOVE STORY

MAINTAINING THE HEDGES AROUND YOUR HEART

It's never too late to recall the details of your early love, but the longer you go without doing it, the easier it is to forget. By telling our stories over and over through the years, we solidify in our minds the things that attracted us to our mates in the first place. That's a powerful, positive way to nurture romance.

TAKE ACTION

Call your parents, grandparents, or a close friend, and ask them to share the story of how they met. Reflect on the joy in the storyteller's voice. Talk about what you've heard. How is it similar to your own tale, and how is it different?

NURTURING THE HEDGES OF YOUR HOME

"We were married in downstate Illinois and left the next day to drive across the country for a job in Washington state," Jerry writes. "So we spent our first honeymoon night at the Holiday Inn in Peoria. It didn't seem at all funny then, but that gets the biggest smile today when we recount our story."

TALK IT OUT

1. What is the funniest moment you remember as a couple? What makes you laugh?

2. Write out some of your craziest moments as a couple. Discuss how to pass your love story on to your children.

3. What was your honeymoon like? What went very wrong and very right?

4. Recall major events—a child's birth, a baby's first steps, a child's first day at school.

PLANTING NEW HEDGES

"I vowed to make Dianna laugh," Jerry writes, "which I have tried to do daily for nearly two decades. (If I've failed by the end of the day, I sometimes resort to swinging from the chandelier.)" Humor can keep a couple sane even during tough times.

1. List ways you've brought a smile to your spouse's face.

2. Discuss openly with your spouse about what brings each of you pleasure in the bedroom.

3. Talk over whether the new openness about sexual matters is a good or bad thing for Christian couples.

4. What hedge do you need to plant and nurture to strengthen your relationship?

COUNTING THE COST OF IGNORING HEDGES

Make your love story so familiar that it becomes part of the fabric of your being. It should become a legend shared through the generations. Grow a family tree that defies all odds and boasts marriage after marriage of stability, strength, and longevity. You can succeed with properly planted hedges.

Think about the sweet love story from Song of Solomon 2:10-14:

> "My beloved spoke, and said to me: 'Rise up, my love, my fair one, and come away. For lo, the winter is past, the rain is over and gone. The flowers appear on the earth; the time of singing has come, and the voice of the turtledove is heard in our land. The fig tree puts forth her green figs, and the vines with the tender grapes give a good smell. Rise up, my love, my fair one, and come away!'
>
> "Oh my dove, in the clefts of the rock, in the secret places of the cliff, let me see your face, let me hear your voice; for your voice is sweet, and your face is lovely."

TAKE ACTION

When was the last time you made overtly romantic overtures to your spouse? Rent a favorite movie, and watch it together in the dark. Find time to read poetry or listen to soft music. Choose to add a dose of romance to your life together. Add fresh sweetener to your love story daily.

Study Guide for Chapter 14

WHEN VICTORY COMES

MAINTAINING THE HEDGES AROUND YOUR HEART

"It's crucial to understand," Jerry writes, "that the hedges I've discussed have been my own, tailor-made for an over-sexed, gregarious, fun-loving, busy person who might otherwise follow his lusts, say things he shouldn't, flirt, forget the most important person in his life, and not spend as much time with his family as he should."

TAKE ACTION

Work with your spouse to list some of the most surprising things you've discovered about yourself through this study. In your own words, explain how the hedges concept could work for you. Note areas where you need to see the greatest improvement in your boundaries. Discuss how your hedges will differ (or be similar) to your spouse's.

NURTURING THE HEDGES OF YOUR HOME

Some couples schedule a breakfast out each week. Jerry knows a pastor and two business executives who have regular appointments with their wives booked right onto their calendars, and their secretaries know those dates are inviolable.

TALK IT OUT

1. Schedule time to get together with your spouse and discuss doing what's necessary to make this happen.

2. Talk about how it makes you feel when a friend or business associate misses an important meeting or phone call. List ways you can keep your spouse a top priority.

3. How do you let your spouse know that she is the most important person in your life?

PLANTING NEW HEDGES

To a busy man, an appointment with his wife on a regular basis is every bit as much of a hedge as Jerry's are to him. Trim your hedges to fit your own life and lifestyle. Spend time talking with your wife. Find out what her deepest needs are, what she really wants and requires from you. Then plant a hedge and make it happen.

TALK IT OUT

1. Discuss signs that would indicate you're heading for a crash. How do you manifest stress to your spouse and family?

2. Talk over with your spouse how you can detect a coming crash and what can and should be done to prevent it.

3. Share with your spouse your deepest needs and heartfelt longings.

4. Determine what each of you can do to help the other find greater fulfillment together.

5. What hedge do you need to plant and nurture to strengthen your relationship?

COUNTING THE COST OF IGNORING HEDGES

Know yourself, understand the dangers in your weak areas, and do something practical and concrete about them.

Consider Ephesians 5:22-33 and its straightforward advice on how a husband and wife should treat each other.

Wives, submit to your own husbands, as to the Lord. For the husband is head of the wife, as also Christ is head of the church; and He is the Savior of the body. Therefore, just as the church is subject to Christ, so let the wives be to their own husbands in everything.

Husbands, love your wives, just as Christ also loved the church and gave Himself for her, that He might sanctify and cleanse her with the washing of water by the word, that He might present her to Himself a glorious church, not having spot or wrinkle or any such thing, but that she should be holy and without blemish.

So husbands ought to love their own wives as their own bodies; he who loves his wife loves himself. For no one ever hated his own flesh, but nourishes and cherishes it, just as the Lord does the church. For we are members of His body, of His flesh and of His bones.

"For this reason a man shall leave his father and mother and be joined to his wife, and the two shall become one flesh." This is a great mystery, but I speak concerning Christ and the church. Nevertheless let each one of you in particular so love his own wife as himself, and let the wife see that she respects her husband.

TAKE ACTION

Remind yourself why you want to remain true to your spouse. Pull out family albums, and go through them as a couple. Review pictures of your children, your happy home, and the fun times you've shared. Renew your commitment to keeping this joy in your life by remaining fully faithful to one another. Seal your promise with a kiss.